Changing Tribal Life in British Orissa

Kanchanmoy Mojumdar

1998

Kaveri Books
New Delhi-110002

First Published in 1998

ISBN 81-7479-026-8

Published by Rakesh Goel
Kaveri Books
4697/5-21 A, Ansari Road,
New Delhi-110002 (India).

Tel: 3288140 Fax:(011) 7198902

Laser Typeset by : Printmedia, New Delhi-110002.

Printed at : Chawla Offset Works, Delhi-110052

PRINTED IN INDIA

For
Rupa and Ranjan

Contents

Preface

The impact of British administration on tribal life of Orissa was both deep and wide. The change effected in the life was the result as much of a policy consciously implemented by the Government as of the force of circumstances not directly caused by any administrative measure. The policy evolved through varied experiences of local administrators charged with the task of "civilising the savages" by conciliatory measures, if possible, and coercive ones, if necessary. The tribal reaction to administrative measures varied between stubborn resistance and grudging acquiescence, depending on the nature of the aboriginals in particular tracts and the means adopted by local authorities to implement the Government's policy.

Initially, British tribal policy lacked even a proper understanding of tribal psyche, let alone a sympathetic appreciation of tribal susceptibilities. The "do-gooders" were determined to "improve" the barbaric aboriginal life according to their own understanding of improved level of living. The Government's laws and regulations were often in conflict with cherished tribal traditions of which the administrators had full knowledge but for which they showed scant deference—unlike all rulers of the tribal tracts before. For long British tribal administration was such as to cause conflict of interests between the Government and its tribal subjects. Even contact with the tribals, essential to control them, had to wait till the British government subdued the men by arms. Contact thus effected did not bring the tribals any closer to the administration.

Later, however, the administrators learned through their experience that the success of their measures required a reconciliation between the needs of the Government and the expectations of a people who had no earlier experience of subjection to a regular administration and who, in fact, had for centuries been the least governed of all the Indian people. The Government would now carefully regulate the pace and extent of change in tribal life and closely monitor its course, the guiding maxim being to preserve "tribalism" to the extent possible.

By the time the British government adopted this new line of tribal policy, the aboriginals had been rendered a harmless and emasculated people, resigned to a life, irreversibly changed by an alien administration; they had put up with forces which they could neither easily internalise nor defiantly ignore. By then, both by temptation and threat the British government had turned a section of tribals into agents of change and collaborators. A peaceable people, the tribals were now looked upon as "noble savages", protected wards of the Government to be cared for by local administrators and insulated against all forces which were potentially or actually harmful to the interests of the colonial government.

Tribal administration under the British *raj* left both a lesson and a legacy for administrators of tribal tracts in post-colonial Orissa. The lesson was : the determined drive to improve tribal life resulted inevitably in progressive detribalisation, ultimately ending up in the irrelevance of tribal administration itself. The legacy was : the awareness that the critical factor in tribal administration was how the channels of change in local life functioned, not what the policy-formulating process was or what the strands of tribal policy were.

In identifying the cause, course and consequence of British tribal policy in Orissa, I have relied mainly on contemporary Government papers, my object being to view the tribal problem of the past through the eyes of those who faced and sought to tackle it. In fact, the most important aspect of the problem underlying the British administration of tribal tracts persists even today : how to "modernise" the tribal life without destroying in the process the distinctiveness of tribalism. Nowhere is the conflict between tradition and modernity so acutely focussed as in tribal administration. British administration in tribal Orissa ended when the local people were in a state of transition, the Government hoping to preserve tribalism after itself generating forces which progressively caused detribalisation.

I owe much to many institutions for having allowed me access to the materials used in this work; a list of these institutions is given in the bibliography. The idea of working on the tribals of Orissa struck me first when I taught at Berhampur University, Orissa for nine years (1968-77) and when I helped some research students working on tribal administration in British Orissa. I recall, in particular, having gone through the great volume and variety of source materials collected by Dr. T.E.R. Iyengar and Dr. Dasarathi Swaro and then having decided to work on the tribals myself.

Comments made on my paper on the Kandh tribe of Orissa at the Australian National University, Canberra and later on another paper on the same tribe at the Davidson College, North Carolina, USA proved helpful. To Professor Prabodh Kumar Mishra of Sambalpur University, Dr Prasanna Kumar Mishra of Utkal University, Shri Srinivas Sahu and Dr Ravuri Dhanalaxmi, once my students at Berhampur University, I express my gratitude for their help in many ways.

I thank the authorities of the Norlin Library, University of Colorado at Boulder, USA for having given me access to the source materials I needed to complete this work. My brother, Hemanta, an anthropologist himself, got me photocopies of many books from his office at Denver, Colorado, without which I could not have executed the work in the USA as smoothly as I did.

Kanchanmoy Mojumdar

Abbreviations

BJCP	Bengal Judicial (Criminal) Proceedings
BPC	Bengal Political Consultations
CC	Chief Commissioner of the Central Provinces
DPI	Director of Public Instruction, Madras
FPA	Foreign Department Political A Proceedings
FPP	Foreign Department Political Proceedings
GC	Ganjam Collectorate Correspondence
HC	Home Department (Public) Consultations
HP	Home Department (Public) Proceedings
HRPO	*History of the Rise and Progress of Operations for the Suppression of Human Sacrifice and Female Infanticide in the Hill Tracts of Orissa*
JOH	*Journal of Orissan History*
MJP	Madras Judicial Department Proceedings
MPSRO	Madhya Pradesh State Records Office, Nagpur.
NAI	National Archives of India, New Delhi.
SDO	Sub-Divisional Officer
SRGC	Selections from the Old Records of the Ganjam Collectorate

Glossary

Batta	Allowance
Bethi	Unpaid labour
Bissoyi	Headman
Bhogra	Rent-free land tenure
Dalbehera	Leader of militia men
Desh	Circle of villages
Dewan	Minister
Gaontia	Village headman
Ghat	Mountain range
Gonda	Village Watchman
Jhankar	Village official to look after the local deity
Jumma	Assessment
Khalsa	Crown land
Kulta	Oriya Immigrant farmer
Majhi	Headman
Maliah	Highland
Maliko	Headman
Mamul	Goods given free
Meriah	Object for sacrifice
Mutha	Village
Muthadar	Chief of villages
Naik	Leader of militia men
Paik	Militia man
Panchayat	Village Council
Pandhari	Road Tax
Patmajhi	Chief of village headmen
Patro	Headman
Podu	Cultivation by slash and burn
Sardar	Tribal Chief
Sowcar	Moneylender
Sundhi	Distiller of liquor, liquor contractor
Umrao	Headman of a circle of villages

1

Studying the Tribal History of Orissa : Perspective, Problems and Prospects

Studies on local tribes are a comparatively new trend in historical research in Orissa. The men, constituting almost a quarter of the population of the state, have traditionally been the subjects of study by anthropologists and ethnologists. However, the results of such study are yet to be fully made use of by historians, for there is a deep-rooted feeling that the tools of historical research and those of anthropological and ethnological enquiry are different, as also the methodology adopted in the three disciplines; and, therefore, historical studies on tribes would necessarily have nothing in common with studies on the same tribes by anthropologists and ethnologists.

This feeling needs to be abandoned, especially when trans-disciplinary approach to issues and events is the latest trend in scholastic activities. Such an approach has established the correlation between several disciplines so that the results of researches in one discipline could be helpful for researchers in other disciplines. A historian tracing the course of change in tribal life over a long period identifies those features in tribal character which the anthropologist may find as the unchanging trait in the character and which influence the mind of the tribals even today. Historians explaining the tribal reaction to alien influences on their life in the past could provide a clue to the present tribal reaction to forces which might still be viewed by them as alien. Thus, historical studies on tribal life, tribal administration in the past and experiences of officers in tribal tracts many decades ago could prove helpful for those dealing with the tribals now.

Source materials for historical studies on the tribes of Orissa are yet to be utilised adequately; and this is mainly because of the fact that the materials could be found at no one place. They are, in fact, located at many places from where different parts of the present-day Orissa used to be ruled at different times. To add further to the difficulty is the fact that a large part of Orissa was for long held by princes who ruled states inhabiting tribals. Materials to write on these tribals are not easy to procure.

Tribal history of Orissa could be studied broadly in its three aspects: one, a critical review of the British government's relations with some major tribes of the state, the circumstances in which the relations were forged and the different phases of the relations. This aspect of the study would bring out the basic problem of tribal administration—determination of the extent of accommodation expected of the tribals, and the degree of imposition considered necessary by the administrator. Secondly, the changing pattern in tribal life over a period of time could be a theme of absorbing interest, highlighting, as it would, the extent, the pace and the channels of the change. In tracing the course of change in tribal life, the historian would find that the administration prevalent in tribal tracts released forces which the local people could neither ignore for long nor effectively resist. The problem of acculturation and attempts at its solution by the tribals themselves deserves intensive study. This might help in model-building by historians, the model to be applied for studying similar problems faced by tribes in other parts of India. Thirdly, the inter-relations between tribal and non-tribal communities in a specific period of time and at a particular geographical area could also be a theme worth studying by historians. The cultural influence affecting the way of life of the tribals and non-tribals living in the same area as cheek by jowl had indeed been a two-way traffic. Such cross-cultural influences could be exemplified by a study of local institutions and their changing character over the ages.

The very nature of the study of the changing cultural life of the tribes would call for a trans-disciplinary approach. While the foundation would no doubt be provided by facts of history, for the sake of a broader and correct perspective, familiarity with such disciplines as social anthropology, sociology, ethnography and economics would be desirable; for the historian has not only to assess the impact of a policy consciously adopted by the government over a definite course of time, but he has also to identify the influences working unobtrusively on the tribal mind over a far longer period of time. Government's policy changed the tribals' material life, but indirect influences changed the tribal psyche, though the process had been far slower and far less obvious. The economist in the historian would look for changes in the living standard of the aboriginals, while the social anthropologist in him would trace the changing way of life of the men.

An analysis of the growth, functioning and decay of tribal institutions and an understanding of their changing nature over a period of time would need a finely balanced and welded outlook of a historian, a social anthropologist, a sociologist and an economist. What is needed in tribal history is not just collection of facts and faithful documentation but interpretation of issues by a sensitive mind with a view to bringing out the changing ethos of tribal life. The extensive historical data would require close analysis with the integrated approach of a historian, a sociologist and an anthropologist.

The inter-relations of the three disciplines in tribal studies cannot be over-emphasised. Historical data could help the anthropologist to buttress his arguments to explain the functional aspects of tribal social institutions and to present thereby the changing pattern of relationships and norms of social behaviour among the tribals themselves and between them and non-tribals. Conversely, social anthropologist's field studies would contribute not a little to the reconstruction of tribal history in its most recent phase. In fact, in the tapestry of tribal study, if history is the warp, sociology and anthropology are the woof.

A comprehensive study of tribal culture in its synchronic and diachronic aspects, in which the anthropologist is interested, would be facilitated by historical research which would establish the fact that culture is a continuing way of life influenced by both palpable and imperceptible forces. To trace the forces and record their impact is the historian's job. In fact, the social anthropologist's task of discovering general laws underlying the growth of tribal institutions would be impossible without some historical data of the recorded period. Historical studies on the tribes of Orissa would thus be complementary to sociological and anthropological studies on them. For the anthropologists it would be of immense interest to compare their own experiences in dealing with the tribes with those of administrators several decades ago.

The focal point in historical studies today is the socio-economic aspects of life, and the factors influencing their development and decay. These aspects in either tribal life in general or with reference to a particular tribe deserve intensive study to explain, among others, issues such as tribal revolts, migration of tribesmen from their habitat, non-tribal "colonisation" of tribal tracts and detribalisation. Of these issues, tribal revolts in several parts of Orissa have attracted some interest among researchers in history; but then, there is still the need for identifying a pattern in their causes, course and consequences. Particular incidents such as the Kandh outbreak in Kalahandi,[1] the *fituri* in Kutiya Kandh tract of the Ganjam Agency[2] and the tribal uprising in Bamanghaty[3] have been studied by scholars, but these apparently unconnected events had better been viewed as a phenomenon, the recurrence of which was due to forces released by an alien government as well as by factors unrelated to the government's policy. Identification of the socio-economic dimensions of these patently political events would help in the construction of some models which the social anthropologist may find useful. This model building would turn out to be a very worthwhile exercise if tribal revolts in Orissa are analysed in comparison with like incidents in other areas of tribal India.

Detribalisation followed acculturation of tribals with non-tribals, its extent, form and pace determined by the degree of acculturation. At times the government's policy had much to do with detribalisation; at others the government had no control on its course and consequences. Detribalisation was, in fact, a stage in the evolution of life in tribal tracts, its pace determined at times by unobtrusive forces, not government's measures. An overall view of detribalisation over a long course of time in the entire tribal tract of Orissa would require the application of minds of historians, anthropologists and sociologists, the latter two for the sake of conceptualisation of events and issues set out by the former.

Socio-economic changes in tribal life could be best traced if the aboriginals are viewed as constituents of a peasant society exposed to what Verrier Elwin deplored as the increasingly "debasing contact" with modern civilisation. The monetisation of tribal economy, the development of market and its effect on the local agrarian life, the replacement of the traditional community ownership of property by individual proprietorship, the breakdown of the village organisation and such other matters—all indicating the process of modernisation—merit close study to explain the persistent feature of tribal life : contact of tribal and non-tribal value systems result in a conflict between them.

Studies on leadership in a community constitute a new dimension in Indian historiography, involving cooperation between historians and sociologists and an interchange of their respective tools of research. Tribal leadership is an interesting theme, especially when studied in the context of an enquiry into the extent of collaboration accounting for the consolidation of non-tribal influences in tribal tracts and progressive detribalisation. British administrators in Ganjam tribal tracts, for example, reared a non-tribal, mainly Oriya, elite, using them as the main catalysts in local tribal life.[4] The traditional tribal leaders progressively lost their accustomed power and position; naturally enraged, they provided leadership to the resultant tribal outbreaks. The British government made the fullest use of the Oriya elite to deal with the outbreaks, and this had a far-reaching effect on the tribal psyche. In course of time tribal leaders too veered closer to the British government and moved farther from their traditional position in tribal society and polity.

A comparative study of different groups of one tribe living under the same administration, but in different tracts, would establish that the impact of the administration was not identical everywhere, notwithstanding the identical object of the measures undertaken by the administrators. The Kandhs of the Ganjam Agency[5] and those in the Kandhmals[6] could be studied together to bring out their different reaction to the same administrative measures of the British government. The Ganjam Kandh's reaction to the Government's educational programme for example, could be compared with that of the Kandhs of the Kandhmals. Both the diversities and unifying features of the Kandh life could be highlighted in a comparative study of the Kandh response to the same "civilising" measures by the same administrative agencies in different Kandh tracts of Orissa. Perhaps more worthwhile would be a comparative study of the Kandhs and Savaras in the Ganjam Agency to explain their respective problems of adjustment to forces released by the alien British administration. A pattern might emerge out of these problems and the course of adaptation to the new unfamiliar forces. This pattern then could be made use of in studying similar problems faced by other tribal groups in other parts of the country ruled by the same British authorities. In fact, tribal administrators of different places exchanged notes, and their respective experiences served both as lessons to follow and as risks to avoid. British tribal policy evolved through the accumulated experiences of officers serving in many tribal tracts.

One common refrain in all official reports on tribal tracts of Orissa is the progressive change in tribal character. Local officers observed that changes in the material life of the aborigines brought about changes in their moral behaviour.[7] An analysis of the changing tribal character on the basis of verifiable and recorded data left by policy makers in the past could be a historian's contribution to the general literature on tribal life, and this could well be utilised by anthropologists to explain the present behaviour of the tribals. Historical facts need to be remembered by the social anthropologist to explain the evolving tribal life and institutions. Indeed, critically analysed historical data could as much reinforce his findings based on observation in field studies as they could also help him correct his own views based on conjectural history.

The historian should view tribal culture as an integrated and unitary system, and tribal society as a centripetal element in tribal culture. Tribal institutions, as they originally were, were a means to preserve social cohesion and stability. Each institution had a specific object to fulfil, and, along with others, a common social purpose to serve; the purpose was to regulate the inter-relations of individuals in society and to unite them for a community life. The individual's importance in traditional tribal society stemmed from his being a component of the community as a whole. Tribal political and economic organisations reflected this phenomenon. Even some religious rites and rituals had as their main motivation the well being of not individuals or families performing them but that of the entire community.

The role of Christian missionaries as an agency of change in tribal life is well known, but not enough has yet been written about it in Orissa.[8] This could certainly be a theme of extensive research, considering the mass of missionary papers that could be made use of. For a historian tribal life as seen by a European missionary and that related by a contemporary official functionary could make interesting comparison. Christian missionaries were no doubt active in tribal Orissa, but their role in the socio-political awakening of the aboriginals in Orissa was in no way comparable to their similar role in, say, Assam and Bihar. A comparative study of the role in the three areas would be a worthwhile academic exercise to explain why the same missionary organisation functioned differently in several tribal tracts, and the results of their operations varied too. Such a study would bring out the regional distinctiveness of tribal reaction to alien influences.

Meriah sacrifice and female infanticide in some tribal tracts of Orissa are the two topics on which a lot has been written by historians of Orissa. Yet, a lot of scope still exists for viewing the two rites as *institutions* having a bearing on the socio-economic aspects of tribal life. How the eradication of what the British government viewed as inhuman practices affected the later growth of tribal mind and life is a question to which historians need to address themselves. It is not enough to just relate the official measures to abolish the practices; it is as much important to analyse the socio-economic consequences of the measures. It is well worth asking why some tribals practised one rite, while some others did not, though all lived in the same tract and had many other things in common. The myths and folk lores woven around these magico-religious institutions could interest the historian and the anthropologist alike. The involvement of some Hindus — both the elite and common men — in the observance of human sacrifice in some tribal tracts is a point of considerable significance as is the collaboration of a new tribal elite, reared by the British government, in the suppression of the practice. The official papers of the "Meriah Agents" are yet to be thoroughly analysed by historians who have almost invariably relied on two published collection of reports[9], besides published memoirs of Campbell[10] and Macpherson[11], to write on the eradication of the practice of human sacrifice.

The original reports of the Meriah officers, to be had mostly in the Home (Public) Department Proceedings at the National Archives, New Delhi, would make useful reading, containing as they do a clear profile of the tribal institutions in the mid-nineteenth century. The officers differed both in their perceptions of tribal problems and in their solutions. Some were over-enthusiastic; others not zealous enough; some would conciliate the refractory tribals; others would cow them into quiescence. Even high officers, Governors-General and Governors including, held different views on the same problem. Concerted action seemed lacking at times while at others coordination of measures seemed urgent. There were at times conflicting opinions between policy implementing authorities and the resultant confusion in the lower levels of tribal administration. With all this, the Meriah Agency is a fit subject for intensive research.

Records and official papers on tribal administration, missionary accounts of tribes and memoirs of officers who served in tribal tracts have one common refrain : the conflict between tradition and modernity, and the inverse relation between the two. "Civilising" the "savages" was the declared object of British administrators of tribal Orissa, and its result was the progressive loss of traditional tribal values. Indeed, the march of "civilisation" in the tribal tracts was as much an inexorable phenomenon as the resultant loss of cherished tribal values an irreversible trend.

The administrator's efforts to establish an acceptable uniform level of economic and social development for all the people under his charge created an inevitable conflict with his obligation to preserve tribal exclusiveness, the prerequisite to tribal identity. British official papers of the period 1915-1947, in particular, provide interesting data on this problem of the Government's tribal policy. The Government was no doubt worried over the expropriation and exploitation of the tribals by non-tribals, but the latter's intrusion in tribal tracts and their activities had at a time been avowedly encouraged by the Government itself as a means of "civilising" the tribals through contact with the representatives of a superior culture. The Government's problem was how to preserve tribalism while setting in motion forces which tended to fuse tribal life with the non-tribal one. The administrator could hardly hide his regret at what would appear to him as a correlation between "sanskritisation" of the aborigines and the erosion of those very values which the "savage" men had practised for centuries but which the agents of "sanskritisation" themselves had lost for ages.

This aspect of tribal study has an immense potentiality, if a comparison is made between the evolving tribal life in Orissa during the British rule and that in other parts of India in the same period. The result of such a comparative study could be valuable for even tribal administrators today, who, like their predecessors, confront the same basic problem : how to reconcile the Government's policy of tribal welfare with the tribesmen's own idea of what is best suited to their interests. A historian's probe into the past would be worthwhile if he could in the process identify the lines of past tribal policy which are relevant to the present and which could in some way be a lesson for the future. An understanding of the proper perspective of tribal study would help historians in both explaining the problems inherent in the study and making the most of its prospects. The use of historical study of tribes lies in this : periodically looking back over the past might prove helpful in looking forward into the future.

Notes and References

1. Kalahandi was a princely state under the jurisdiction of the Central Provinces administration. See K. Mojumdar, "Revolt in Kalahandi, 1881-82 : Peasant Uprising in a Tribal State," *Osmania Journal of Historical Research,* (Department of History, Osmania University, Hyderabad), Vol. II, Nos. 1 & 2 (Jan. 1983-Dec. 1985), pp. 7-33.
2. Kanchanmoy Mojumdar, *Proceedings of the Seminar on Socio-Economic Life of the Tribals of Orissa During the 19th and Early 20th Centuries,* (Khallkote College, Berhampur, Orissa), 5-6 July, 1981, pp. 25-36. Also published in *New Aspects of History of Orissa,* Vol. III (Dept. of History, Sambalpur University, Jyoti Vihar, 1981), pp. 13-23.
3. Bamanghaty is a tribal tract in Mayurbhanj, a princely state in British Orissa. Tribal revolts occurred in Bamanghaty in the 19th and early 20th centuries. See D. M. Praharaj, *Tribal Movements and Political History of India*

(New Delhi, 1988), pp. 104-28. Also Prasanna Kumar Mishra, *Political Unrest in Orissa* (Calcutta, 1983).

4. K. Mojumdar, "The Ganjam Agency, 1839-1000: Some Problems of Tribal Administration", in P. K. Mishra, ed., *Culture, Tribal History and Freedom Movement, Dr. N. K. Sahu Commemoration Volume* (Delhi, 1989), pp. 154-5.
5. In 1839, the Ganjam Agency was constituted with most aboriginal tracts; Kandhs and Savaras were the main tribal groups in the Agency. The Kandhmals was a Kandh tribal tract under the jurisdiction of the Bengal government. See M. M. Mahapatra, "Changing Pattern of Khond Life—A study in British Impact" in *Ibid,* pp. 141-47.
6. "The Changing Pattern of Tribal Economy in Khandmals—A Study in British Impact" in *Proceedings of the Seminar on Socio-Economic Life of the Tribals of Orissa* (Khallikote College, Berhampur), *op. cit.*, pp. 41-45.
7. See, pp. 64, 121, 140-41 below
8. The only full-length study on Christian missionaries and their deeds in Orissa has been done by Dasarathi Swaro in his work *The Christian Missionaries in Orissa, Their Impact on Nineteenth Century Society* (Calcutta, 1990) There is a chapter in the book on missionary activities among the tribal people.
9. The two reports are *History of the Rise and Progress of Operations for the Suppression of Human Sacrifice and Female Infanticide in the hill tracts of Orissa* (Calcutta, 1854) and *Reports of the Meriah Agents (Ganjam) from 1837 to 1861* (Madras, 1885).
10. J. A. Campbell, *A Personal Narrative of Thirteen Years Service Among the Hill Tribes of Khondistan* (London, 1864).
11. William Macpherson, *Memorials of Service in India : from the Correspondence of the late Major Samuel Charteris Macpherson, C. B. political agent at Gwalior during the Mutiny, and formerly employed in the supression of Human Sacrifice in Orissa* (London, 1865).

2

Tribal History of Orissa : A Study in Archival Source Materials

Research in tribal history has rich potentialities, considering the vast and varied archival source materials on which to draw it. The importance of such materials can hardly be over emphasised. For any history to be authentic it needs to be based on facts culled from written records. The degree of reliability of a historical work is determined by the depth of its foundation in verifiable facts, and the verifiability itself has a direct relevance to the extent to which the facts are recorded. Hence, an authentic history of tribal Orissa needs to be based on definite and verifiable records, the earliest of which are, roughly speaking, a little more than two hundred years old.

Although governments in Orissa in the pre-British period knew of tribal people, dealings with them did not constitute an important element in state policy; one is not even certain if pre-British governments in Orissa compiled any state papers concerning the tribals; such papers, if at all compiled ever, are difficult to obtain for historical research. In contrast, the British government in Orissa was not only aware of the tribals but had a definite policy to deal with the problem they created for the administration. Necessarily, therefore, an authentic tribal history of Orissa would relate to the period which marked the growth of this awareness and the implementation of this policy.

But then, writing the history of tribes in British Orissa is not an easy job, for the vast archival source materials have to be diligently collected from records offices in several states. Until 1936 there existed no province of Orissa having in it all the Oriya speaking people. Parts of western Orissa, with a large tribal population in them, were under the government of the Central Provinces and Berar; the administration of the tribal areas of Ganjam and Koraput districts of south Orissa was the charge of the Madras government. The Kandhmals in the district of Angul was a part of the Bengal administration, while tribes of the many tributary states of Orissa were reported on by Superintendents of the Tributary States of Orissa; the reports were regularly sent to the Government of India, and at times to the governments of Bengal, Madras and C.P. and Berar. Tribal administration had several levels—local, sub-divisional, district, provincial and central; and so government records created in all the levels and dealt with them by different authorities should be closely studied for the complete profile of tribal administration to emerge.

Besides, not all the tribal tracts of Orissa came in British contact at the same time, nor was the contact uniform in character to create among all the aborigines an impact of identical intensity. British control of tribals following their contact with the men was not equally effective in all the regions. In many regions the adoption of a definite policy towards the local tribes followed many years after the Government acquired some knowledge of them. For example, although British officers serving in Ganjam since the 1760s,[1] when it came under the British possession, knew of the local Kandhs, a definite policy to deal with them did not emerge till about seven decades later. This would explain why there are only a few records on the Kandhs pertaining to the pre-1830 period, while records of the later period could be had in plenty. Thus, the necessity of adequate documentation would restrict the scope of a definitive history of tribal Orissa to post-1830 period.

The Kandhs of Ganjam created disturbances in the last decades of the 18th and the early decades of the 19th centuries. Ganjam district officers reported on these incidents; and so grew the old Ganjam papers on the local tribes; a printed index of these early reports is available. But the short description of the Kandhs in these reports are mostly second-hand information, there being at that time no regular British officer in the Ganjam Kandh tracts.

For a fuller account of the tracts and their inhabitants, their society, religion, economy and political set up, one has to wait till the 1830s, when George Russell, the First Member of the Board of Revenue, Madras, wrote a comprehensive report on a section of the Kandhs of Ganjam[2]. The report outlined a tribal policy which for many years served as the guide and manual for later administrators of Kandh tracts. On

Russell's recommendation, the Agency administration was set up in Ganjam hill areas; and it lasted for about one hundred and twenty five years from the 1830s.

The Agency records constitute the most important primary source material to reconstruct the history of tribal administration in the districts of Ganjam and Vizagapatam. First-hand reports of officers in charge of the different parts of the tribal tracts in the two districts, the Agents' tour diaries, comments on the reports and diaries by Governors and Councillors and the measures adopted for tribal administration, all these are found mostly in the Judicial Proceedings of the Madras government, in the Tamil Nadu archives.[3] Annual reports on the administration submitted by Agents and their subordinates, all printed, are particularly important. In the Ganjam and Vizagapatam collectorate record rooms, one could trace many papers dealing with the Agency tracts, the papers being mostly hand-written; the authors were subordinate staff of the Agency administration. Ganjam and Vizagapatam Agency papers, dealing with the Savaras and Kandhs mainly, could be used to compare tribal administration by Madras authorities with that by Bengal and C.P. administrators.

A part of the Ganjam and Vizagapatam Agency papers, formerly preserved in the Tamil Nadu state archives, Madras, were made over to the Orissa and Andhra Pradesh governments when the two new states came into being. The Ganjam tribal papers, so transferred, lay in the records room of the Ganjam collectorate at Chatrapur for many decades till about twenty years ago they were shifted to the Orissa State Archives at Bhubaneshwar. The papers, some hand-written and some printed for official use, were in a very bad state of preservation when they were transferred to the Orissa State Archives. Happily, however, some important papers on tribal administration were printed by the Madras government in its Judicial and Revenue Proceedings, and they could be had in the Tamil Nadu archives. The annual administration reports on tribal tracts in various provinces were printed by the Government; they contain excellent summary of events in all the areas of the tracts and the measures adopted at various levels of the tribal administration.

The voluminous papers of the Orissa Hill Agency or the Meriah Agency[3a], as it was also called, could be found in the Home (Public) Department papers of the Government of India at the National Archives. The Meriah Agency functioned under the direct control of the Government of India in the Home Department. The reports of the officers of the Meriah Agency, some of which were printed by the

Government, contain intimate details on the political, social and economic implications of tribal socio-religious practices and the measures adopted by the Government for the social reclamation of the tribesmen. The very exhaustive report on the working of the Meriah Agency by J.P. Grant (1848) following the Kandh outbreak in 1846 makes interesting reading. In some Judicial Department Proceedings of the Madras and Bengal governments, there are copies of reports of the officers of the Meriah Agency.

Government papers on the tribals of Kalahandi, Sonepur, Balangir-Patna and other states of western Orissa are available in the Foreign (Political) Department Proceedings in the National Archives; also in the same proceedings are available administrative reports on the Kandhmals, for long a part of the Angul district. The princely states of Mayurbhanj and Keonjhar had a large Santal population; the changing life of the Santals was reported upon by the Superintendent of Orissa tributary states; these reports could be had in the Political Department Proceedings of the Bengal government in West Bengal State Archives, Calcutta. The private archives of former princely states of Orissa and estates of Parlakhemundi and Jeypore are worth a close search for a proper appraisal of tribal policy. Tribal life in tracts of British Orissa merits comparison with that in princely states[4] and zamindaries; in the latter tribal disturbances took place due to maladministration; and the paramount British government had to intervene to redress some glaring grievances of the tribals.

Tribal disputes on lands under two administrative jurisdictions were settled by officers deputed by the two authorities, and so the cause, the course and consequences of the disputes could best be studied in the records of the two administrative headquarters. For example, disputes on tracts bordering Boud and Ghumsur were settled by officers of the Kandhmal sub-division under the Bengal government and those of the Ganjam Agency under the Madras administration; hence, records pertaining to these disputes should be looked for in the Ganjam collectorate records office and the Angul district records office. Kandhs of the Kalahandi state and the Savaras of Jeypore created problems for the administration by their frequent affrays with their neighbouring tribes to settle disputes on land. Papers on these disputes could be studied in the Tamil Nadu archives, the National Archives and the Madhya Pradesh Secretariat Record Room at Nagpur.

Tribal outbreaks often assumed wide ramifications despite the British government's determination to localise them. The researcher has to study relevant papers in more than one archives to reconstruct the origin, the developments and results of these events. Thus, for the suppression of the Kandh outbreaks in Ganjam in 1836-37, 1857 and 1865, the rebellion of Chakra Bissoyi in 1846 and 1855-56, the Savara disturbances in the Ganjam Agency in 1853 and 1856, and Kalahandi Kandh uprising in 1881, the authorities of the Madras, Bengal and C.P. governments acted in close concert. Comprehensive reports on these outbreaks and the measures taken to suppress them were printed by the Government for official use and circulated to all the authorities involved in the issue.

Social and economic impact of the British rule on the tribes of Orissa is an interesting study, for which one needs to consult not only annual administration reports on tribal tracts under provincial governments but also look up papers in the proceedings of the Financial, Public Works and Revenue (Special) departments of the governments. Some political measures of the British rulers produced important social results. For instance, a new tribal elite gradually emerged whose power stemmed more from the alien Government's encouragement than from the customary support of fellow tribals. The more the British rulers made use of the elite to manage the tribals, the more powerful they became and in consequence more oppressive too. There are numerous records to trace this development as also to observe that tribals eventually resisted the trend, obliging the Government to restrain the elite.[5]

Demand for tribal workforce for the construction of roads, for watchmen for Government rest houses, for forest guards and teachers in schools in tribal tracts brought into being a class of men, economically dependent on the British government and serving as purveyers of new influences among the tribal people. The resultant acculturation between tribals and non-tribals is referred to in the annual reports on tribal tracts of all the provinces in British India.

The changing economic life in Kandh tracts was noticed by T. E. Ravenshaw, the Commissioner of Orissa :

> The Khonds formerly possessed little property of any sort. A red cloth or brass plate was rare. Now-a-days in most of the more respectable houses you see brass vessels in tolerable profusion. They have acquired considerable wealth in silver and

> brass ornament; and where they formerly went half-starved and half-naked, they have now abundance of food and liberal supply of raiment. Cultivation is extended and they grow large quantity of cotton, oil seeds and turmeric for export.[6]

The Kandh tracts referred to by Ravenshaw were under the Bengal government; The Kandhs under the Madras administration, living mostly in Agency tracts, had not attained in the 1880s any comparable economic level, which is clear from the reports of the Agents of Ganjam and Koraput tribal tracts. The changing economic life of the tribals has been referred to in the proceedings of the Financial, Public Works and Revenue (Special) Departments of the Madras government. The social implications of the economic change merit analysis by researchers.

The government's determination to control shifting cultivation with a view to preventing the progressive denudation of forests, to restrict consumption of forest products by the local people and to extend the areas of reserved forests for ensuring the adequate supply of sleepers for railways were new economic measures which created not a little annoyance in tribal mind. The Government also sought to check the manufacture and consumption of liquor by the tribals as a means of preventing drunken brawls, besides heavy indebtedness and impoverishment through mortgage and sale of lands to non-tribal money lenders.[7] The Judicial Proceedings of the Madras government and the government of the Central Provinces contain a lot of facts on this point as do the Political Department Proceedings of the Bengal government; but for more details one needs to look up papers in the Revenue (Forest), Development, Finance (Separate Revenue) Departments, and the Proceedings of the Commissioners of Excise and the Board of Revenue.

Proceedings of the Education Department of different governments dealing with tribes and those of the Director of Public Instruction clearly suggest that the high hopes underlying the establishment of schools in tribal tracts were not met, for not the tribals, but non-tribal immigrants made the most of the schools.[8] These immigrants often acted as the collaborators of the Government officers and exploited the tribesmen. Tribal reaction to Christian missionary educational programme in Orissa could be compared with that to the Government's efforts to spread education in tribal areas; and for this missionary literature constitutes an invaluable source material. The spread of education in Bihar and Assam tribal tracts and that in Orissa tribal areas could be studied together on the basis of archival source materials with a view to comparing the successes achieved by the respective governments and failures suffered by them.

Not all the tribal tracts in Orissa had the same pattern of change nor did the changes effected by the British government follow an identical course. The Kandhmals, for instance, posed, generally speaking, fewer problems for local authorities than the Kandh tracts in the Ganjam Agency and those in the fuedatory states of Western Orissa. A study of the records of the Kandhmals in West Bengal archives, the Agency records of the Ganjam and Vizagapatam districts in the Tamil Nadu archives and papers on the Kandhs of western Orissa in M.P. Secretariat Record Room at Nagpur and the National Archives would enable the researcher to compare and contrast the activities of tribal administrators under several provincial governments and the varied local reactions caused by the activities. Sometimes the experience of officers in one tribal area proved helpful for those in another area who faced identical problems. Thus, the measures adopted in the Kandhmals to prevent alienation of tribal lands to non-tribals provided a guideline to the Ganjam Agency officers to deal with the same problem in their area.

Archival source materials contain facts to clearly suggest that tribal administration in all areas had one basic problem : effecting changes in tribal life without destroying in the process its distinctiveness; bringing modernity to the people while avoiding an overt conflict with their age old tradition. Tribal desire to go their accustomed way had to be reconciled with the determination of the non-tribal administrator to bring about the moral and material development of the people in accordance with the existing ideas of benevolent administration.

Notes and References

1. The British acquired Ganjam from the Nizam of Hyderabad in 1766 as a part of the Northern Circars. It was a district of the Madras Presidency till 1936 when it was transferred to Orissa, a new province that was created in that year.
2. *Reports on the Disturbances in Parlakimedy, Vizagapatnam and Goomsoor in 1832-36* (2 Vols.) in *Selections from the Records of the Madras Government XXIV of 1856* (Madras, 1856).
3. Tamil Nadu Archives is in Madras.

3a. Human beings whom the Kandhs sacrificed to propitiate the earth goddess for the maintenance of the fertility of their land were called *Meriah* by the Oriyas of the tribal tracts, although the Kandhs called them *Toki* or *Keddi*. Macpherson, *Report Upon the Khonds of the Districts of Ganjam and Cuttack* (Calcutta, 1842), pp. 62-67. Rev. W. Taylor, "On the Language, Manners and Rites of the Khonds", *Madras Journal of Literature and Science*, VII (Madras, 1837), pp. 43-44.

4. See pp.122-23 below.

5. See pp. 36-37, 41-42, 64, 79, 115 below.

6. Quoted in E. T. Dalton, *Descriptive Ethnology of Bengal* (Indian Edn., 1974).p 301. The report was dated 1871.

7. K. Mojumdar, 1989, *op. cit.*, pp. 157-60.

8. See p. 120 below.

3

The Kandhs of Ganjam, 1836-1861 : British Impact on a Tribal Society

The British government came in close contact with the Kandh tribe of Ganjam in 1836 when a military expedition was sent against it. The year 1861 saw the abolition of a special agency which the Government had set up in 1845 for suppressing the practice of human sacrifice and female infanticide prevalent widely in some Kandh tracts.

During the period the first hand knowledge acquired of the tribal tract, the local people, their religion, society, economy and general way of life enabled the Government to gradually adopt a policy of bringing the Kandhs under the "civilising" influence of the British rule. The policy passed through several phases of experimentation, of trial and error. It provoked considerable reaction in the tribesmen; it affected several segments of their society in different ways. For the Kandhs contact with the British government was an exposure to a unique influence which could neither be easily assimilated nor ignored for long. It caused them the natural problem of adjustment to a new situation. True, in just fifteen years the tribal society had undergone no remarkable transformation, but surely new catalytic forces had been set in motion to provide the dynamics of change in the traditional tribal life.

British relations with the Kandhs of Ganjam were a sequel to the measures taken by the Government to put down rebellious *rajas* of the Ganjam hill tracts.[1] Captain John Campbell, who served in the Kandh tracts for thirteen years between 1836 and 1854, found the *rajas* "exceedingly proud and haughty" and "devoid of all mental culture, an abjectly degraded class".[2] The *rajas* on their part, intensely disliked the British administration with its rigid rules and regulations which, as some

British officers admitted, were often at variance with the time-honoured local conventions and practices. All earlier rulers, the Mughals, the Marathas and the Qutb Shahis of Golconda, who held sway over different parts of Orissa, had, infact, treated the hill chiefs as feudatories and semi-independent princes rather than as mere zamindars or landlords. Until the British rule the chiefs had generally been left alone, their only obligation being to pay—and that with no regularity—a small tribute to the paramount power. They had never paid so large a tribute nor as regularly as the British demanded. In fact, irregular payment of tributes to the paramount authority was for the chiefs a recognised practice; the British government viewed it as wanton defiance of its authority and clear sign of recalcitrance.

British administration of Ganjam affected the traditional interests of the local hill chiefs; much of their powers and privileges were gone. They lost their customary judicial and police authority and the right to nominate successors. Their forts were demolished and armed retainers disbanded. Many estates were attached by the Government and many more auctioned. In the *rajas'* familial quarrels the British government intervened, its policy being to back the party which promised it the largest tribute. This intensified dissensions among the local aristocracy, caused deterioration in their administration and provided the Government with greater scope and justification for intervention. Evidently, as a British officer admitted himself :

> No consideration was given to the character of these ancient zamindars which rendered it impossible to expect that an aristocracy so rude and powerful should at once conform themselves to the exigencies of the new system.[3]

Soon the discontent among the hill chiefs and their subordinates—the *patros, bissoyis, malikos, dalbeheras* and *paiks*—would spark off a general tribal revolt, the Kandhs' traditional loyalty to the chiefs and the latter's incitement accounting for it. All the men would rally behind the discontented chiefs, determined to defend the traditional and accustomed political set up. The British recognised it themselves:

> The fixed restrictive rule of the Government was necessarily extremely burdensome to a race accustomed to the fast-and-loose administration of a native authority which they themselves swayed, and they have desired the restoration of that authority as the means of regaining their lawless freedom.[4]

Military expeditions against the Kandhs and the hill chiefs would then follow, the Government having resolved to set an example of ruthlessness to strike terror in the tribal mind. Fields with standing crops and sometimes even entire villages would be set on fire, youngmen publicly hanged and leaders brutally tortured and exiled for life. Such ruthlessness did no doubt quell the disturbances but not bring the tribesmen any closer to the Government. Nor at first did the Government even aim at that, its object being just to deepen fear in the Kandhs to exact their quiescence and deference to authority; the Government at first had no intention of effective and regular administrative control of Kandh tracts. Such control was, in fact, rather difficult to secure, the climate being too unhealthy for prolonged stay of Government officers in tribal tracts and communication facilities practically non-existent. The British government would levy no tax on the Kandhs, for so long they had paid none at all to any.

However, the policy of let alone could not be continued for long, for it was at variance with another strand of-British policy : prevention of cruel social customs and religious rites which were repugnant to humanity. The British in India assumed the role of social redeemers, and as such they viewed the traditional Kandh institutions. No sooner were they aware of the practice of human sacrifice and female infanticide in Kandh tracts than they took steps to suppress them. But then, the policy of social reclamation of the tribals proved difficult to implement until the Government could effect a closer political and administrative control of the Kandh tracts.

Human sacrifice among the Kandhs was both a social institution and a religious rite, suggesting a close identity between the ecclesiastical and temporal interests of the tribesmen. It was a means of propitiating the earth goddess whose favours were needed to maintain the fertility of the soil. It was also a form of public expiation to the anger of the goddess to avert droughts, epidemics and natural calamities. The rite was celebrated as a public oblation by the entire tribal community or some brances of the tribe; it thus helped in the maintenance of community spirit in the tribesmen. The Kandhs believed that the blood of the victim caused the redness of the turmeric, an important crop of the tribal tract, and his tears brought the rains.[5]

The victims could be male or female, their age varying from six months to sixty years. They were always purchased from the *panas*, who procured them from destitute families in the plains. The price was paid in livestock, brass vessels and even land. The victims were called *meriah* in Oriya, although the Kandhs called them *toki* or *keddi*. A Hindu priesthood, called the *jani*, was associated with the rite of human sacrifice in Kandh tracts as were the *paiks, bissoyis* and *patros*, the latter receiving a sum of money when the rite was performed. Even Oriya hill chiefs, though Hindu, performed human sacrifice to secure divine blessings when they assumed power or wished to avert danger.[6] For the Kandhs human sacrifice "was an act of worship ... the very essence — the vital fact of their superstition-forming, in one point of view, its very sum"[7] It was to them a "national and most necessary duty",[8] intimately associated with their economic life and its well being.

Female infanticide was prevalent in some Kandh tracts where as many as twelve hundred girl children were killed every year. Marriage of daughters involved payment of bride money by parents who naturally disliked girls as a financial burden. Besides, women were an important element in recurrent tribal disputes which served to deepen the prejudice against them. The destruction of life and property in the disputes following the capricious dissolution of marriage ties by Kandh women made the practice of female infanticide rather a cruel necessity for the Kandhs.[9]

Although the British government was keen on putting a stop to these cruel practices, it took time to adopt an effective policy to do so. Generally speaking, the Government's efforts, until 1845, were "partial, unconnected and unsustained".[10] Thereafter, the efforts were "combined, sustained, continuous and systematic".[11] British officers engaged in the suppression of human sacrifice and female infanticide in Ganjam Kandh tracts were of two categories : one, like George Russell, J. P. Frye, J. Cadenhead and John Macpherson, who would generally avoid using arms against the tribals and instead exert moral pressure on them to wean them from the cruel practices; the other, like John Campbell, A. J. Mills and J. R. Ousley, who sought to achieve the object by keeping alive the Kandh dread of the Government caused by earlier punitive expeditions. In the end, both the means were tried, conciliation and coercion, each as a complement of the other.

For several years after 1836, when Russell sent his first report on the human sacrifice and female infanticide in Ghumsur,[12] an estate in the Ganjam district, the Government's general policy was just to persuade the Kandhs to give up the prospective victims and to rehabilitate the rescued *meriahs* at public expense. British officers toured the Kandh tracts to obtain first hand knowledge of the tribesmen and exert personal influence on tribal leaders. In meetings arranged with the latter, undertakings were obtained that the practices would be dispensed with.[13] The Government hoped that truthfulness and fidelity to public engagements being the two notable elements in Kandh character,[14] pledges by tribal leaders would well serve as commitment by all their followers.

However, the policy of moral influence and persuasion alone did not yield much result, although victims for sacrifice were periodically obtained from tribal leaders.[15] Even pecuniary grants to the leaders and assurance of Christian missionaries to enlighten the Kandhs on the cruelty of their socio-religious rites did not prove very effective, for, as the *Friend of India* observed:

> Bribery was powerless when people believe a crime to be their greatest earthly gain and moral suasion seems impracticable when applied to races who would consider a missionary an acceptable offering to the gods.[16]

What, in fact, the Government needed to do was to convince the Kandhs that the observance of the two rites had no relation whatever with their economic prosperity and social stability. And this could best be done, as British officers dealing with the Kandhs soon realised, by utilising the influence of the Oriya aristocracy on the tribal people and the traditionally intimate relations between the two. The Government then adopted a new policy, the "key stone" of which, as Campbell recognised, "was the conquest of the Oriya chiefs without whose aid and cooperation it would have been as easy to have built a city in the air as to have suppressed the human sacrifices amongst the Khonds".[17] The Oriya aristocracy were tempted with rewards if it cooperated with the Government and threatened with punishment if it did not.[18] As it soon turned out, the British government's measures in tribal tracts were effective to the extent the local Oriya aristocracy could be motivated in the Government's civilising mission.

In 1845 the Government set up a special establishment to suppress the two inhuman practices in the hill tracts of Orissa. Called the Orissa Hill Agency or the Meriah Agency, it was vested with authority over the entire tribal tract which until then was under the administrative jurisdiction of the governments of Bengal, Madras and the Governor-General's Agent for the South-West Frontier States. The one controlling authority now established promoted better coordination among officers, unity of action by them and speedier execution of policy. The new

Agency was under the direct control of the Government of India; the first Meriah Agent was Captain Macpherson.[19]

Macpherson showed an admirable combination of prudence, flexibility and firmness in dealing with the Kandhs. He established direct personal contact with Kandh chiefs, seeking to lay hold on "the reason, the feelings, the prejudices and the material interests" of the men. In dealing with them he gave "a fair trial to every conceivable expedient in the way of peaceful conference, persistent argument, humane conciliation and honorary reward".[20] But then, if all the peaceful means failed, he would punish, though lightly, all those who broke the common engagement to refrain from the rites.[21] He sought to create in the tribesmen an opinion against the rites and to use the opinion to increase his own influence in the tribal tracts.

From now on the authority of the tribal chiefs and the Oriya aristocracy and the moral influence of the British officers would coexist in Kandh tracts. The fighting propensity of the hill chiefs and their retainers was now considerably restrained; their authority was "humanised" and allied to that of the British officers. It served a two-fold purpose : first, it committed the Oriya aristocracy to the success of the Government's measures. The *patros* were now made "the first and the most essential link in the chain of responsibility" within which the Government sought to enclose "every party of influence in the land."[22] Secondly, the importance of the Oriya aristocracy allied to the Government as collaborators was a new development in the tribal society. These men helped in the gradual emergence of a "strong anti-sacrificing party",[23] the means by which the Meriah Agency accomplished the task of bringing the tribals under its moral tutelage.

Generating confidence in the Kandh mind by dispelling their dread of the Government was the key to the success of the Meriah Agency's measures. Proclamations were periodically issued, disclaiming any intention of the Government to levy tax on the tribal people, and guaranteeing the customary rights and privileges of tribal leaders.[24] The Government did not even want to abolish the practice of sacrifice as such; all that it wanted was the substitution of human beings by buffaloes and goats. Agency officers did not want to be viewed as "imperious innovators"; they reposed trust in the tribesmen, for they found it better "to place confidence in the Khonds when there is no reason to doubt their sincerity than to distrust them."[25]

Officers like Frye and Cadenhead sought to know the Kandhs better by learning their language and conversing with them in it. Frye gave the

Kandh language its first written character, using the Oriya script; he translated Christian religious texts into the Kandh language.[26] Gradually British officers' influence in tribal tracts increased, the local people at places having been attached to them. The traditionally exclusive relations of the Oriya hill chiefs with their tribal subjects were now broken, British officers interposing their authority between the chiefs and their subjects.

The Government was keen on creating in the Kandhs "a sense of benefits" from contact with and subjection to the British rule.[27] Markets and fairs were set up near the Kandh tracts to facilitate easier communication between the tribals and the people of the plains. A semi-military security force was raised from among the hillmen, the recruits being mostly *paiks,* the landed militia who served the hill chiefs.[28] Meriah Agency officers kept registers of the rescued *meriahs* who were committed to the care of influential tribal leaders.[29] A small number of schools were set up in the Kandh tracts in the 1850s which served to sow in local minds "the first seeds of intellectual and spiritual desire."[30] Roads were constructed not only "as the surest and most efficacious means of introducing civilisation amongst barbarous races, but as the death blow to rebellion".[31]

British contact with the Kandhs caught the latter between compulsions of tradition and ineluctable forces of change. British administration of the tribal tract produced in course of time its natural results. The tribal propensity to settle disputes by arms was gradually curbed; frequency of feuds, skirmishes and military expeditions having diminished over the years, an element of stability was introduced in the tribal political structure. In course of time the Government could not only turn the Kandhs into peaceable subjects but also convince them that the Government's interest lay in promoting tribal welfare.

British administration brought in its wake a change in the concept of land-ownership.[32] Contrary to tradition, membership of a clan was no longer the only title to land nor could new lands be acquired by arms. Now the Government was the new source of local authority and power, and it guaranteed retention of property as the surest means of maintaining peace in Kandh tracts. The Government would resist the tradition of land-grabbing by arms. *Patros* were held responsible for the maintenance of law and order in Kandh tracts; any dereliction of this primary responsibility on the part of a *patro* resulted in his replacement by another, more amenable to Government control and more effective as a peace keeper. Thus new hill chiefs, new *patros,* new *bissoyis* and new *malikos* came into being, all tied to the Government by obligation, their title to power being its recognition by the Government and their tenure dependent on their service to the Government.[33] The Kandh *sardar* was gradually overshadowed by the new Oriya elite as the intermediary between the tribesmen and the British government. The traditional balance between the Oriya aristocracy living for generations in tribal tracts and the Kandhs got disturbed when the former's close association with the Government enabled them to wield much more power and authority than ever before.[34] The Oriya aristocracy became increasingly detached from the Kandh socio-religious tradition and general way of tribal life in proportion as their links with the non-tribal subordinate staff of the local administration became stronger. For the old generation of Kandhs the Oriya elite favoured by the British government were indeed a disruptive force, for they were the means of changing tribal life.

British rule had one more result : by the end of the nineteenth century the customary link between the Ganjam hill chiefs, their retainers and the tribesmen was not much of a problem for the Government; strong measures against a refractory hill chief or his subordinates did not lead to a tribal uprising in his support as before.

British administration met one "great and pressing social want" in Kandh tracts : "justice peacefully administered." [35] British officers arbitrated in tribal disputes and dispensed justice; they established a "civil jurisdiction capable of determining society to order"[36] where earlier the society was "everywhere distracted by contests, animosities and feuds".[37] The Government took into consideration most of local customs and conventions before making innovations and at times made use of tribal leaders to reinforce its authority. For the dispensation of justice the joint agency of tribal leaders and Government officers was essential, for, as Macpherson explained :

> We are to attempt chiefly by engrafting our authority upon the institution of the tribes to give them justice not only as an end but as a chief means of acquiring the dominion over them which is necessary to effect our objects.[38]

The Government would prevent disputes between individuals from escalating into fights between clans.

British contact with the Kandhs exposed the latter to a larger and different society as also to new economic forces. Their economic frontier continued to expand in proportion to changes in the social frontier.[39] Their means of livelihood tended to get more diversified. They worked as labourers to make roads; some of them became small traders; some served as watchmen in Government rest houses; some came down to the plains to earn some money. Visits of Government officers gave some impetus to local trade of the Kandh hills. The tribesmen gradually got over their fear of British officers; a time came when Kandh men, women and children trekked many miles to reach the officers' camps to sell local products and to procure from the officers beads, mirrors and red cloth, which they prized much.[40]

The British government's policy was to create in the Kandhs new wants, and to lay hold on their economic life so as to bring the tribals closer to the administration. The Government encouraged the traffic of non-tribals to Kandh tracts, particularly traders.[41] In course of time Kandh habits tended to change when at fairs and markets set up by the Government they could get things for which earlier they had to depend on the *panas.* Some Kandhs could now hope to get better price for the things they sold in local markets besides buying things more cheaply than before. By suppressing the *meriah* rite the Government prevented the tribesmen from an unprofitable investment, for every *meriah* had to be dearly bought.[42] But then, despite the Government's effort to convince the Kandhs that the *meriah* rite was an "impoverishing falsehood", the desire for the revival of the rite persisted in Kandh mind; it surfaced in times of epidemics and scarcity of crops.[43] Fear of punishment by the Government alone prevented the recurrence of the rite, not any conviction of its irrelevance to the economic life of the tribal community.

The spread of Christianity in Kandh tracts led to the emergence of a new social group. The evangelical work of the missionaries went hand in hand with education and moral reclamation of the Kandhs[44]. Officers of the Meriah Agency encouraged the missionaries to live in tribal tracts as agents of moral improvement of the local people, thus furthering the Government's policy. For the rehabilitation of the rescued *meriahs* the Government relied on the missionaries who took charge of these "government children"; the Government provided an allowance for the latter's maintenance.[45] In mission schools, *meriah* boys learned tailoring, weaving, printing and book binding, while to the *meriah* girls was taught housewifery. The missionaries at times helped some boys in finding employment which took them away from their accustomed society.[46]

However, education, the best means of effecting social change, did not spread among the Ganjam Kandhs either as fast or as widely as the Government desired. The Kandhs feared that the establishment of schools was but a prelude to assessment of land and realisation of land tax by the Government.[47] In 1855-56 there were only fourteen Government schools in the Kandh tracts of the entire Madras Presidency in which 147 pupils were enrolled; of them only seventeen were Kandhs, and the rest Oriyas.[48] However, matters improved a little in later years when tribal chiefs could be coaxed to take some interest in schools set up in their tracts. In 1860-61 the progress of the schools was reported to be "very satisfactory", with 521 pupils enrolled in them.[49] Lack of trained teachers willing to serve in wild tracts was the most serious impediment to the Government's educational programme in Kandh tracts.[50]

Most Kandh children left their studies soon, and those who did not, later migrated to the plains for their livelihood. They gradually lost contact with hill life; they imitated Hindu habits, observed Hindu socio-religious rites and tended to get merged in low caste Hindu society, having been accepted as low caste Hindus by the local people. These Kandhs developed a new outlook, new loyalties and a new view of life; very little of the traditional Kandh set up survived in their descendents. For the Kandh tracts this was indeed a social loss, for in these few educated and enterprising tribals lay the potentiality of the growth of a new leadership in tribal society.

Notes and References

1. For almost seventy years from 1766, when Ganjam came under the British government, the local *rajas* intermittently rose against the government. T. J. Maltby, *The Ganjam District Manual* (Madras, 1918), pp. 148-50; T. E.R. Iyengar, "Resistance to British rule in Ganjam, 1766-1858" (Unpublished Ph. D. thesis, Berhampur University, 1976).
2. Campbell, 1864, *op. cit.*, pp. 26-7. Home (Public) Consultations (hereafter H. C.), National Archives of India (hereafter NAI), 7 October 1858, No. 157.
3. D. F. Carmaichael, *Manual of the District of Vizagapatam* (Madras, 1869), p. 228. See also Maltby, 1918, *op. cit.*, pp. 89-153.
4. HC, 7 Oct. 1858, No. 124, Cadenhead to Macpherson, 22 Dec. 1846.
5. *History of the Rise and Progress of Operations for the Suppression of*

Human Sacrifice and Female Infanticide in the Hill Tracts of Orissa (Calcutta, 1854—hereafter HRPO), pp. 3-4, 10, 40-46. S. C. Macpherson, "An Account of the Religion of the Khonds of Orissa", *Journal of the Royal Asiatic Society of Great Britain and Ireland,* XIII (1851-52), p243

6. J. P. Frye, "On the Uriya and Kondh Population of Orissa", *Journal of the Royal Asiatic Society of Bengal"*, XVII (1859-60), p. 19. Carmaichael, 1869, *op. cit.*, p. 348. Dalton, 1974, *op. cit.*, p. 290.
7. Quoted in Anonymous, *Calcutta Review,* VIII, Nos. XV & XVI (July-Dec. 1847), p. 5.
8. Campbell, *op. cit.,* p. 51.
9. Bengal Judicial (Criminal) Proceedings (hereafter BJCP), 19 June 1843, No. 101. HRPO, pp. 46-9, 66-8. See pp. 45-58 below.
10. BJCP, 19 June 1843, No. 101, Macpherson to Bannerman, 31 May 1843.
11. Anonymous, *op. cit.,* p. 2.
12. From 1766-67 till 1836, the Ghumsur ruling family, the Bhanjas, and the local zamindars resisted the consolidation of the British rule in the region till, following the disturbances in the tract, the estate was taken over by the British government. The Bhanja rule ended there. The Kandhs, forming a large segment of the local population, always assisted the ruling family in its revolt against the British authority. Iyengar, *op. cit.,* pp. 82-127.
13. HRPO, pp. 13-5, 55-7.
14. Macpherson, 1851-52, p. 52.
15. *Campbell, op. cit., pp. 265-6.*
16. 28 September 1854.
17. Campbell, *op. cit.,* p. 261. Frye, *op. cit.,* p. 32.
18. H. C. 31 Mar. 1849, No. 15
19. BJCP, 18 Mar. 1846: Resolution of the Home Department, Govt. of India, 6 Dec. 1845.
20. Rev. Dr. G. Duff, "Goomsur: The Late War There; The Khonds or Wild Tribes", *Calcutta Review,* 1846, p. 105.
21. HC, 7 Oct. 1848, No. 124.
22. Frye, *op. cit.,* p. 32. HC, 7 Oct. 1848, Nos. 70, 90, 92.
23. William Macpherson, *op. cit.*, p. 189.
24. BJCP, 18 Nov. 1846, Nos. 156-7; 20 Nov. 1850, No. 77. HC, 7 Oct. 1848, No. 154.
25. BJCP, 19 Nov. 1851, No. 131 : Secretary, Home Deptt., Govt. of India to Secretary, Judicial Deptt., Govt. of Bengal, 17 Jan. 1851.
26. *Ibid.,* 11 Sept. 1850, Nos. 165-7, HC. 21 July 1849, No. 26. Barbara M.

Boal, *The Konds : Human Sacrifice and Religious Change* (Warminister, Wilts, 1982), p. 75.

27. BJCP, 18 Mar. 1846, No. 210 : Resolution of the Home Deptt., 6 Dec. 1845.

28. BJCP, 19 June 1843, No. 105 : Home Deptt. Minute, 31 May 1843.

29. HRPO, *op. cit.*, pp. 130-31.

30. Govt. of India, Home (Public) Letters to Court of Directors, No. 58, 11 October 1852. S. Pearce Carey, *Dawn on the Kond Hills* (London, 1936), p. 24.

31. BJCP, 1 July 1844, No. 100 : Hills to Secretary, Judl. Deptt, 1 June 1844.

32. F. G. Bailey, "Political Change in the Khondmals", *The Eastern Anthropologist,* XI, No. 2 (Dec. 1957-Feb. 1958), p. 92.

33. HC, 7 Oct, 1848, No. 157.

34. Bailey, *op. cit.*, pp. 96-7.

35. HC, 7 Oct. 1848, No. 90 : Macpherson to Grant, 23 Sept. 1847.

36. BJCP, 19 June 1843, No. 102 : Macpherson to Bannerman, 15 Aug. 1842.

37. *Ibid.*

38. *Ibid.;* also HC, 7 Oct. 1848, Nos. 77, 90.

39. F. G. Bailey, *Caste and Economic Frontier : A Village in Highland Orissa* (Manchester, 1957), pp. 5, 9.

40. Frye, *op. cit.*, p. 14.

41. Govt. of Bengal Political Proceedings A, July 1863, No 15.

42. The price varied between 50 and 100 "lives"—a sheep, a cow, a pig and a fowl being a "life". Macpherson, *Report Upon the Khonds of the Districts of Ganjam and Cuttack* (Calcutta, 1842), p. 64.

43. As late as 1954, Verrier Elwin, who knew the aboriginals of Orissa intimately, having toured through their tracts several times, found the Kandhs still longing for human sacrifice. See his *Tribal Myths of Orissa* (London, 1954), pp. XXV, 692-3.

44. Carey, *op. cit.*, p. 36. *The Calcutta Christian Observer* (Apr.-July 1837).

45. BJCP, 14 Mar. 1837, Nos. 128-9; 4 Apr. 1837, Nos. 19-20; 24 Dec. 1845, Nos 202-203.

46. *Ibid,* 21 July 1840, No. 46; 19 Jan. 1848, No. 121.

47. *Reports of the Meriah Agents (Ganjam) from 1837 to 1861* (Madras, 1885), pp. 52-6.

48. Govt. of India Home (Public) Letter to Court of Directors, No. 67, 18 August 1854 (NAI). *Reports on the Administration of Public Affairs in the Madras Presidency for the year 1855-56* (Madras, 1856) pp. 37-8.

49. *Ibid, for the year 1860-61* (Madras, 1861), p. 128. But the number of Kandh

pupils in the schools is not given in this report.

50. On the educational programme and the problems in its implementation see pp. 120-21 below.

4

The Ganjam Agency, 1839-1900: Problems of Tribal Administration

Essentially, the main problem of tribal administration is one of reconciling the conflicting interests of the many people covered by the administration. This involves a process of adjustment of relations between the Government and the tribesmen, between the latter and their leaders, between the tribals and non-tribals, and not unoften even between the various agencies of the administration itself. The fact that these agencies operate at various levels of the administration creates another problem : how to coordinate the agencies to ensure their efficacy.

British administrators of the Ganjam tribal tracts were indeed solicitous for the moral and material uplift of the local people, but they also recognised that their zeal for tribal welfare often scared the men, for their accustomed life had been affected by administrative measures of an alien Government. The rulers' zeal for tribal welfare proved incompatible with the fondly cherished tribal values. In such circumstances, the administrators had to formulate such a policy as, while meeting the growing needs of the Government, would avoid any direct assault on tribal traditions.

British policy in the Ganjam hill tracts had three dimensions, all closely inter-related : suppressing the periodical tribal revolts, the adoption of measures to "civilise" the tribals, and protecting them from the exploitation of non-tribals, the exploitation being coeval, commensurate and co-extensive with the consolidation of the British rule in tribal tracts.

The geographical features of the Ganjam tribal tracts, the nature of the local people, and the peculiarities of their society and polity were factors which influenced the local British administration. The highlands of Ganjam, called *maliahs* covered 3,500 square miles of territory out of the total 8,311 square miles of the area of the district. 3,138 square miles of the *maliahs* were in the 19th century inhabited by aboriginal tribes, mainly Kandhs and Savaras.[1] The Ganjam administration in the 19th century was often hard put to prevent the spread of local tribal discontent to the contiguous tribal tracts of Vizagapatam and Jeypore as also to tribal tracts in Chattisgarh feudatory states and those under the Bengal Presidency.

The Ganjam tribal tracts had dense forests, swamps and hills interposed with fertile valleys. So rugged, difficult and unhealthy most of the hill tracts were that, let alone the British, even people of the adjacent plains could not live there at any time except the cold season of about three months from December.

The tribals of Ganjam were at various stages of civilisation, the extent of contact with non-tribals determining the stage, and the extent itself depending on the geographical proximity of the tribal tracts to areas inhabited by non-tribals. The tribals living in hills were farther from civilisation than those living in the foothills where exposure to extraneous influences was easier.

There were three important features in the tribal psyche, polity and society which had a bearing on the British government's policy. First, the strong spirit of independence in the tribesmen fostered by the local geographical features, and the absence of any regular and rigid local administration for ages. In fact, the men were used to no close administrative control, for none had ever been attempted by pre-British rulers. Secondly, local *rajas* and zamindars, all Oriya Hindus, and their hirelings formed an integral element of the tribal socio-political structure. Traditionally, the Oriya aristocracy held but a loose political sway on the local tribal people, their subjects, exercising influence rather than exerting strong authority and power. The Oriya aristocracy recognised the independent spirit of the tribesmen and avoided interference with their cherished institutions, particularly the customary privileges of tribal leaders.

An intimate and interdependent feudal relationship subsisted between the Oriya aristocracy and their tribal subjects. The former received free service and free supply of local products from the latter. Originally, this unpaid service and free gifts were but a token of tribal regard for and loyalty to the Oriya elite, but in course of time they tended to develop as symbols of the elite's domination of their tribal subjects. The Oriya *rajas* and zamindars had scarcely any direct, regular and intimate relation with their tribal subjects; such relations were maintained by the *patros* and *bissoyis* who managed the tribal tracts with the help of their armed retainers, the *paiks*. The *patros* and *bissoyis*, besides maintaining law and order in their respective spheres of authority, mediated in tribal disputes in accordance with local customs and conventions. The tribal chiefs, called *muthadars*, had to work in cooperation with the Oriya *partos* and *bissoyis;* no written laws and regulations governed tribal society, but customs and usages were strong enough to hold the society together. The Oriya elite in Ganjam hill tracts were involved in endemic internecine feuds in which were drawn their tribal followers too. Some Oriya *rajas* and zamindars though Hindus, performed distinctly tribal rites and rituals while some *patros, bissoyis* and *paiks*, living for ages among the tribals, actively participated in their social and religious functions and festivities.

Tradition had a very strong hold on the tribal mind, and any administrative measure affecting it provoked tribal reaction. The Oriya elite's position and influence in tribal society was based on a clear recognition of this basic fact. British administrators of Ganjam tribal tracts learned the hard way that assault on tribal tradition led invariably to tribal discontent and revolt.

The strong traditional tie between the Oriya elite and their tribal subjects made it inevitable that measures that hurt one would set off reaction in the other against the administration that took the measures. The problem of dealing with the Oriya elite bore within it the problem of dealing with their tribal subjects and *vice versa*; through out the course of the Agency administration, the two problems remained intertwined.

Tribal outbreaks in Ganjam in the 19th century were often the sequel to the strained relations between the refractory Oriya *rajas* and zamindars on the one hand and the British government on the other; campaigns against the Oriya aristocracy led to armed conflict with their tribal subjects.

It was in 1836, during a military campaign against the refractory *raja* of Ghumsur that the British government came in direct contact with his tribal subjects, the Kandhs. The hunt for the fugitive *raja* sheltered by the Kandhs escalated into a full-scale war against the tribesmen. Ghumsur, one of the six important estates of the Ganjam district, had a long tradition of defiance of the British authority ever since it was established in Ganjam in the 1760s.[2] The campaign against the Ghumsur *raja* and his Kandh subjects led to the adoption by the

British government of a definite policy to deal with the tribals of the Ganjam district. The establishment of a special administrative machinery was the first step towards the implementation of the policy.

By Act 23, 1836, the Ghumsur and Surada zamindaries with their tribal tracts were removed from the jurisdiction of ordinary regulations and placed under the special administration of the Collector of the Ganjam district who was given the additional designation—Commissioner; he was vested with summary civil, criminal and revenue powers in the tribal tracts that formed his special charge. An army officer, designated the Assistant Collector, would help him in administering the tribal tracts in times of emergency.[2a] George Russell, the Special Commissioner sent by the Madras government to deal with the Ghumsur crisis, made it clear that the tribal administration could be effective only if the Government stepped up its influence in what had hitherto been a virtual *terra incogmita*. Contact with the tribals was the first step to control them.[3]

Russell referred to not only the problem of law and order alone but also to the need for socio-religious reclamation of the Kandhs. It was during the Ghumsur campaign that the Government acquired a first hand knowledge of human sacrifice and female infanticide practised by the Kandhs. The two inhuman practices the Government was determined to abolish, and a special measure was adopted for the purpose. By Act 24, 1839, the Ganjam Agency administration was set up, the entire tribal tract of the district having been brought under its jurisdiction.[4]

The Act superseded the earlier 1836 Act and removed all the hill areas of the district from the operation of ordinary regulations and placed them under the special authority of the Collector of Ganjam who was to function, in respect of the hill tracts, as Agent to the Governor of Madras. The Agent would administer both civil and criminal justice. The Assistant Collector, Ganjam, designated the Principal Assistant to the Agent, was to help the latter in administering the hill tracts by undertaking periodical tours in them to establish contact with the local tribal people and prevent human sacrifice and female infanticide in their tracts. So came into being the Ganjam Agency; The Government would bring about a change in the accustomed life style of the Kandhs and Savaras, the main tribal groups, but that only gradually. Extending civilisation among the barbarous people was as important an object of the new administrative measure as strengthening the Government's authority and influence over them.

However, despite this new measure, the Government found it hard to "humanise" the tribals, whose socio-religious beliefs had strong enough roots to withstand the steps the Government took to destroy them. The Kandh conviction persisted that their agricultural prosperity depended on the continuance of the performance of human sacrifice. The tribesmen attributed the periodical failure of crops to the discontinuance of the performance at places at the Government's instance. The Kandhs wondered why the Government banned the rite when it knew well that all the victims were purchased and none by either coercion or temptation. What the Ghumsur Kandhs grudged the most was the fact that Kandhs in Baud and Daspalla continued to perform the rite of human sacrifice while the Government had banned it in the Ganjam Agency.

This indeed was the fact; the Gumsur Kandh's grouse was fully justified. Baud and Daspalla, both feudatory states, were not under the Madras administration but under the Bengal government whose officers had not been as zealous to wean the local Kandhs from the rite as the Madras officers serving in the Ganjam Agency had been. This made the Government of India aware of the urgent need for coordinated efforts and concerted action by officers posted in all the contiguous tribal tracts of the Bengal and Madras Presidencies to stamp out the rites of human sacrifice and female infanticide. Accordingly, in 1845, the Government of India set up a new administration, called the Orissa Hill Agency or the Meriah Agency, the latter name being linked with the victims of the rite, called locally, *meriahs.*

The Meriah Agency functioned under the direct control of the Government of India till 1861 when it was wound up. The tribal tracts under its jurisdiction were restored to their respective parent authorities. The tribal tracts of Ganjam reverted to the jurisdiction of the Ganjam Agency administration.

The Meriah Agency fully justified its creation; the public performance of human sacrifice and female infanticide gradually ceased throughout the extensive tracts covered by the Agency administration. The Kandhs substituted buffaloes for human beings to propitiate the earth goddess. The Government acquired an intimate and first hand knowledge of the tribals, their life and living, their customs and observances, their history and heritage, and this knowledge profoundly influenced the Government's later tribal policy.

Meriah Agency officers' reports convinced the Government that tribal administration involved not just controlling a savage people by punitive measures but of winning the trust and confidence of simple races who for centuries had lived outside the pale of civilised society and who were unused to subjection to close administrative authority. The Meriah Agency officers' long and close contract with the tribals established the fact that the simple aboriginal people responded far more favourably to personal and paternalistic rule than to bureaucratic and authoritarian governance. And its best evidence lay in the perpetuation of the names and deeds of some British officers in the legends and folklores of the tribals themselves.[5] A sympathetic understanding of the susceptibilities of the tribals was the most enduring legacy of the Meriah Agency.

The Government hereafter followed a three-fold policy : weeding out the local elements which still opposed the Agency administration; creating and strengthening a class of local collaborators in tribal tracts; and setting up institutions with a view to gradually effecting socio-economic changes in tribal life.

In the festering discontent among some Oriya *rajas* and zamindars of the district lay the smouldering embers of local hostility to the Agency administration. These men and their underlings, the *patros, bissoyis* and *paiks*, continued for long to be unreconciled to the British authority which sought to curb their warring proclivities and compelled them to pay regular tributes; confiscation of their estates further intensified their bitterness, driving them at times to armed revolts against the Government. These men made common cause with some tribal leaders who grudged the Government's ban on the performance of human sacrifice. The coalescence of the disgruntled Oriya aristocracy and discontented tribal leaders caused the Government considerable worry. Between 1853 and 1857, the Savaras of Parlakhemundi, a large estate in the Ganjam district, rose in revolt under the leadership of local discontented *bissoyis.* At the same time troubles flared up in Ghumsur where Chakra Bissoyi, a local leader attached to the old, dispossessed local zamindar family, had his own scores to settle against the Government. Chakra Bissoyi won over the Kandhs by promising them the revival of *meriah* sacrifice. The wild Kutiya Kandhs also rose in arms in 1865, registering their defiance of the Government by the public performance of human sacrifice.

All these challenges to its authority the Government met militarily and politically. Troops tore into tribal tracts, shattering the myth of their inaccessibility. Exemplary punishments were meted out to many defiant tribal leaders and Oriya *patros, bissoyis* and *paiks*. The Government rewarded the men loyal to them by recognising them as the new *patros* and *bissoyis* on their undertaking to help implement the Government's tribal policy. Thus was raised a new Oriya official elite tied to the Agency administration by obligation and gratitude; it was the Government's recognition that provided legitimacy to the position acquired by the new elite and not the traditional allegiance of the tribesmen which had been the base of the replaced Oriya elite's position in tribal polity and society. Significantly enough, many rescued *meriah* boys were entrusted to the care of loyal *patros,* who provided them with some gainful employment; some meriah *girls* were given in marriage to Kandh chiefs who were trusted by the Government. [6]

The mission to civilise the tribesmen led the Agency administration to open schools and dispensaries in tribal tracts; fairs and markets were set up to facilitate economic mobility and roads were constructed as the chief means of opening up the tribal tracts as also the tribal mind.[7] The tribal fear that the Government would impose a land tax on them was allayed by a clear proclamation by the Meriah Agency that the Government had no such intention[8]—and the British government honoured the pledge till it lasted. This, more than anything else, convinced the tribals of the good faith of the Government and its sense of justice and fair play. No doubt, it helped in the pacification of tribal tracts.

The new official Oriya aristocracy was the main instrument of the Government's tribal policy; the new *patros* and *bissoyis* were the veritable maids of all work; they had to personally attend to the needs of Agency officers; they were accountable for any breach of law and order in the areas under their charge; they were responsible for the functioning of schools, dispensaries, post offices, markets and above all, for the construction and maintenance of roads and communication links.

With added responsibility, the Oriya elite assumed more power. The power corrupted soon as reflected in the ripples of tribal discontent at many a place. The Government's general policy was one of inactivity until the development of a grave law and order crisis following the wanton abuse of power by the Oriya elite. Periodical tribal disturbances in the second half of the 19th century did not, of course, result in any great change in tribal administration, but they did stimulate probes into it and brought about the redressal of some immediate grievances of the tribesmen. An illustration of this is provided by the Kutiya Kandh uprising in 1865-66 when the Government did a stock taking of the existing policy and, finding it defective, adopted some new measures to tone up the tribal administration.[9]

Repression of the revolt was just the immediate step; the Government needed to adopt some long term measures to generate confidence in the tribal mind and attach the tribals firmly to the Agency administration. A fresh approach to the tribal problem was called for; curing the obvious ills of the existing administration was not enough; the Government had to prevent the ills from developing at all. It was now decided that British officers themselves would live in tribal tracts for most of the year, extend their influence among the local men by direct contact with them and summarily settle local disputes to prevent the accumulation of grievances. The Agency administration would now compile exhaustive annual reports on tribal tracts, covering all aspects of the changing tribal life with particular reference to tribal-non-tribal relations. These annual reports constituted reference materials for successive tribal administrators who learned from the experience of their predecessors while charting for their successors the course they ought to follow and warning them against ignoring tribal susceptibilities. The Agency officers would now observe far greater caution and understanding of the tribal psyche.

However, as heretofore, the Government would even now avoid administering the tribal tracts too closely; it would leave the management of the tracts to the Oriya elite, who were now more effectively controlled by Agency officers. Not inability to pay the Government their tributes alone, but inefficiency as local peace keepers led to several Oriya elite's dispossession of their power and position. Some powerful zamindars lost chunks of tribal tracts for the same reason, the Government itself taking over their management.[10]

With the consolidation of the Agency administration and the extension of its activity, a time soon came when a conflict appeared between what the Government considered necessary for the development of tribal tracts and what the tribals viewed as essential for the maintenance of their accustomed way of life. Growing administrative needs and the tribal desire to be left alone had an inherent incompatibility; and this was stressed by Agency officers while reporting on the tribal reaction to the Government's efforts at conserving forests, controlling drunkenness among the tribals and spreading the benefits of education in them.

The traditional mode of agriculture in the Ganjam Agency was shifting cultivation—a process of clearing forests atop hills by burning, tilling the land so cleared for some years, abandoning them thereafter, and then, moving on to other forest tracts to repeat the process. Shifting cultivation resulted in the deforestation of streamheads on hill tops, caused inundation of agricultural fields on foothills and destruction of crops in the plains below the hills. The Government decided to check what it viewed as but wanton destruction of forests, particularly in the catchment areas of the streams for safeguarding irrigation channels by steadying the flow of rivers and checking floods.

Besides, since the Government received no land revenue from most of the Agency tracts, it turned to forest products, particularly timber, as a source of revenue to meet the increasing cost of administration. Accordingly, some forests were declared reserved where shifting cultivation was banned.[11] Local *patros* and *bissoyis*, having found timber trade profitable, prevented the tribesmen from felling trees in some tracts from where they supplied timber to merchants, mostly from Madras. The tribals strongly reacted to what they resented as wanton interference with their accustomed economic right which no Government earlier had questioned. Oriya *patros* and *bissoyis*, being the Government's main instrument in implementing the scheme of conservation of forests, earned the tribal displeasure all the more.

The drinking of locally made liquor was not merely a habit of the tribals but also an essential element in their socio-religious life. Singing and dancing under the influence of liquor and performing religious rites under the same influence was a well-recognised tradition as reported by Meriah Agents. But in the last decades of the 19th century the Government viewed this tribal habit differently : drunkenness was the main cause of crimes in tribal tracts the incidence of which had increased over the years. A large number of *sundhis* or professional distillers and liquor vendors had come to the foothills and even tribal tracts and settled there; they supplied cheap liquor to the local tribesmen. Agency officers noted not only increasing drunkenness among the tribals but the progressive loss of their lands to the *sundhis* who lent money to the men, holding their land in mortgage.[12]

To check this development, the Government introduced excise rules and sought to regulate the supply of liquor through a licensed liquor contractor who sold liquor through authorised shops under his control. This led to illicit manufacture and trading in liquor, necessitating the maintenance of an increased staff to operate the excise rules. The

Government admitted having effected no appreciable diminution in the drinking habits of the tribesmen nor any check in the alienation of their lands to *sundhis;* but financially, the excise administration was not a failure. The Government earned some revenue from the sale of stills and liquor shops set up by the liquor contractor.[13]

Effecting social change by spreading education was a fond project of the Agency administration which was first implemented in the tracts where human sacrifice and female infanticide were practised. The first step the Government took was to allay the tribal fear that imposition of some tax would follow the establishment of schools.[14] But then, the few schools that functioned after 1861, when the Meriah Agency was abolished, were rather a testimony to the Government's perserverance than of its imagination. Only a few Savara and Kandh children went to the schools which had mostly Oriya children, wards of the local elite, as students.[15]

The Government, however, persisted in its educational project. It urged *patros* and *bissoyis* to generate among the local people an interest in education; the Oriya elite were made responsible for the proper functioning of the schools for which the Government provided an inspecting staff. Some scholarships were instituted and grants in aid were provided to schools where students achieved good results. Government officers were given financial incentives to learn the Kandh and Savara languages.[16]

But then, the problems of the school administration defied solution. Tribal students found Oriya difficult to master, and the language of instruction was Oriya; there were but a few teachers willing to work in unhealthy tribal tracts; lack of books and teaching aids was another handicap; above all, the general apathy of the tribal people to education and their inertia accounted for the failure of the Government's educational programme. The Kandhs and Savaras failed to recognise the correlation between attaining an educational standard and the acquisition of a higher economic level by making use of the education. To the tribal mind sending children to fields or even sites of road construction seemed far more gainful than sending them to schools for the prospect of some employment in a distant future.[17]

Another problem of the Agency administration that became acute in the later decades of the 19th century and after was how best to adjust the deteriorating relations between the subordinate staff of the administration and the tribal people, and how to mitigate the oppression of the tribals by the Oriya official elite. Efficiency in the Agency administration led inevitably to the expansion of its scope which resulted in closer links between the Agency staff and the Oriya elite. The subordinate staff of the local administration and the Oriya *patros* and *bissoyis* acted in close concert for enhancing the efficiency of the administration; they often became partners in exploiting the people under their charge. The Government could not easily prevent this development any more than it could let the tribal discontent fester as a result.

The dilemma faced by the Government was best represented in its reaction to the main tribal grievance in the last decades of the 19th century and after : the remorseless exaction of free supplies and free service by the Oriya elite and the subordinate staff of the Agency administration. The tribals did not grudge either *mamul* and *bethi*, for both were customary, but they complained about the ever-increasing volume and variety of the demands made on them. There seemed no limit to the frequency of the demands either. The Government enquiry reports on *mamul* and *bethi* vindicated the tribal grievance that the Oriya elite had indeed taken the fullest advantage of the Government's dependence on them as agents of change in tribal life, and that both the *mamul* and *bethi* which they had been exacting over the years were far more in scale and frequency than warranted by tribal custom and convention.[18]

But then, the reports also emphasised that free supplies and free service to the official Oriya elite were so much an integral element of the Agency administration that their abolition was impossible without impairing the efficiency of the administration itself. They were essential for the preservation of the elite's power and influence in tribal tracts, and this the Government could not afford to let be compromised; much less so when the Government was still disinclined to assume a direct administrative responsibility of the difficult tracts, from where it received practically no land revenue at all. Without *bethi,* in particular, the cost of constructing roads in hilly tracts would be an unaffordable one. The Oriya elite would have to be employed for the sake of the effectiveness of the Agency administration itself.[19]

The system of free labour and free supplies was iniquitous but indispensable. The Government was aware of the economic burden and political risk involved in the abolition of the system; at the same time it was fully alive to the moral impropriety of the system, especially when these traditional institutions were being misused by those whose duty was to promote the moral and material welfare of the tribals.

In such circumstances the Government could do no more than make a compromise between compulsions of administrative needs and the urgency of safeguarding tribal interests. Hereafter the Government would periodically adjust the increasing demands of the Oriya elite for *mamul* and *bethi* with what the tribals would concede as their traditional obligation. The quantum and periodicity of both free supplies and free service would now be carefully determined by the Agency officers after on-the-spot enquiries and in consultation with all the parties concerned. The Agency administration would prevent any great diminution in the local authority and influence of the Oriya elite in the tribal tracts as much as they would stymie any tribal revolt against the elite.[20]

The result of regular, intimate and on-the-spot enquiries into the tribal problems was a gradual change in the Government's attitude towards the tribals. The attitude was one of sympathetic understanding of a people who had just reasons to resent the authority which impinged on their accustomed way of life and to react against the rules of administration which harmed their way of life and to react against the rules of administration which harmed their interests. Ganjam Agency officers traced the reaction of the local men to what they viewed as an unfeeling administration which assumed in later years an exploitative character as well. Change in the tribal life was indeed inevitable, but the Agency administration, by the end of the 19th century, did realise that the change had better be effected as gradually and as imperceptibly as possible, adjusting administrative needs with the susceptibilities of the tribals. The problem was how best to "civilise" the "noble savages", and then how to save them from the concomitant result of the civilisation itself—the propensity of the administration and its "civilising agencies" to exploit the men under their charge. The more the efficiency of the administration, the wider was the scope of the activity of these agencies, and greater was the problem of the oppression of the tribesmen. The Agency administration itself recognised that the test of a good tribal administration lay not in the intention of the administrators at high levels but in the reaction of the local people to the activities of those agencies of the administration with whom the people had to have immediate and direct contact in their day to day life.

Notes and References

1. T. J. Maltby, *The Ganjam District Manual* (Madras, 1918), p. 1. *Madras Manual of Administration,* Vol. I (Madras, 1885), p. 7. On the Kandhs and Savaras see Maltby, *op. cit.*, pp. 52-60, 70-74. E. T. Dalton, *Descriptive Ethnology of Bengal* (Indian Reprint, Calcutta, 1973), pp. 294-312.

2. See pp. 18-19 before. Ghumsur, ruled by the Bhanja family, was one of the oldest zamindaries of the Ganjam district. The five other zamindaries with a large tribal population in them were Athagada, Parlakhumundi, Vijaynagar, Pratapgiri and Mohuri.

2a. *Madras Manual, op. cit.*, p. 63.

3. Russell's *Reports, op. cit.*

4. The Agency was defined as "a tract inhabited chiefly by illiterate animists of nomadic habits addicted to shifting cultivation, observing special religious and ceremonial customs (who) should continue to be administered under the paternal form of government which is identified with the term Agency." GC, 201/1917 : L. T. A. Harris, Agent, Vizagapatam Agency to Govt., 16 Apr. 1915.

5. Campbell and Macpherson, for example, found their place in Kandh ballads and folklores with their names corrupted into local language.

6. *HRPO, op. cit.*, pp. 130-31. *Reports of the Meriah Agents (Ganjam), op. cit.*, p. 45.

7. BJCP, 21 July 1840, No. 46; 19 Jan. 1848, No. 121. Bengal Political Consultations (hereafter cited as BPC), 29 Sept. 1859, No. 5.

8. BJCP, 18 Nov. 1846, Nos. 156-57; 20 Nov. 1850, No. 77. HC, 7 Oct. 1848, No. 154.

9. See pp. 75-84 below.

10. For example, the Government attached some tribal tracts of the estates of Peddakimedi and Chinnakimedy. MJP, Govt. Order, No. 1068, 14 July 1898. Also Ganjam Manual, *op. cit.*, p. 11.

11. GC. D. Dis. 26/1923. Govt. Order, 27 May 1890, Revenue No. 3217.

12. Agency officers observed with concern the "daily increasing degradation and pauperisation of the Kandhs owing to the unrestrained operation of the Sundhis." MJP, Govt. Order, No. 2110, 12 Oct. 1876 : Ganjam Agency Administration Report for 1875-76.

13. *Ibid.* Also *Madras, Manual, op. cit.*, pp. 74-75.

14. Govt. of India Home (Public) Letters to Court of Directors, No. 58, 11 Oct. 1852. S. Pearce Carey, *Dawn on the Kand Hills* (London, 1936), p. 24

15. In the Agency tracts, the Director of Public Instruction, Madras found "the

continued decrease in the number of pupils belonging to the aboriginal tribes." Proceedings of the D. P. I., 19 June 1896.

16. MJP, Govt. Order, No. 1956, 15 Nov. 1889 : J. G. Horsefall, Agent to Chief Secretary, 13 Sept. 1889. Proceedings of the D.P.I., Madras, 28 May 1894, No. 5102. Report on Ganjam Agency Schools, 1892-3. MJP, 7 Nov. 1874, No. 43 : Administration of Hill Tracts, 1873. *Ibid.*, 8 Oct. 1878, No. 2032 : Administration Report of the Ganjam Agency, 1878.

17. See pp. 119-20 below.

18. Report of C. F. MacCartie on the Bissoyis of Parlakhemundi, 24 Nov. 1881. M. Mounsey, *History of the Ganjam Maliahs* (Madras, 1884). M. D. Taylor made an enquiry into *mamul* and *bethi* prevalent in the Ganjam Agency in 1901-02. His Report was reprinted by the Govt. of Orissa in 1949.

19. See pp. 60, 64, 66, 117-18 below.

20. GC. File No. 6756/1926 : Ganjam Agency Office Note on the Evolution of the *Vetti* System.

5

Female Infanticide in the Hill Tracts of Ganjam

Female infanticide in India in the nineteenth century represented man's general prejudice against woman in an extreme form. It was a common practice among the Rajputs of northern, western and central India — a practice which gradually ended not by legislation so much as by education and the general enlightenment that followed it. The practice was also prevalent in some Kandh tribe-inhabited hill tracts of Ganjam.

A study of the literature on female infanticide in the Kandh tracts of Ganjam, both published and unpublished—the latter being mostly Government records—would point to sociological factors underlying the origin of the practice and economic ones influencing its development. And tradition would explain the persistence of the practice through the ages. Admittedly, tenacious adherence to tradition has been as pronounced a feature in Indian social development as, on occasions, a determined defiance of it. Nothing, in fact, illustrates better this dichotomy in Indian social psyche than the Indian man's attitude to woman's permissible position in society.

The motivation to female infanticide among the "civilised" and the "savages" was not absolutely identical, although there was likeness in the factors accounting for its currency. The British administrators' reaction to the practice in both the "civilised" and the "savage" tracts was, of course, the same : a determination to eradicate a glaring social evil by a policy of both persuasion and pressure. However, in the "civilised" regions the eradication was accomplished in about a century, while in the "savage" tracts of Ganjam hills, the administrators claimed to have fulfilled much of their mission in just about twenty five years, 1836-1861, the two terminal dates marking, respectively, the date of launching the operation against the practice, and that of ending it.

In 1836,while leading a military expedition against the recalcitrant zamindar of Ghumsur in the Ganjam district, Colonel George Russell, then the First Member of the Board of Revenue, Government of Madras,[1] chanced upon the prevalence of female infanticide among the Kandhs of Surada, a neighbouring tract. In the next twenty five years, while eradicating the practice, British officers in Kandh tracts of Ganjam collected a mass of facts about it, its origin, operation and motivation, its basis and hold on tribal tradition, and its impact on tribal socio-economic institutions.[2]

In 1845, a special establishment, called the Orissa Hill Agency for the Suppression of Human Sacrifice and Female Infanticide, was set up under orders of the Government of India. For fifteen years thereafter, officers of the Agency sent their reports to, and received their instructions from, the Home (Public) Department of the Government of India.[3] Consequently, records of this Department constitute an invaluable source for the compilation of the history of the ritual-based institutions of the Kandhs of Ganjam.

Enquiries were also made by the Government to ascertain if female infanticide prevailed in the Kandh tracts under the Bengal government and in those in the Nagpur state ruled by the Bhonsles.[4] The results of these enquiries could be had in the records of the Bengal Judicial (Criminal) Department, and in the reports of the British Residents at the Nagpur Court. Copies of the reports filed by officers in the Kandh tracts of Bengal, Madras and Nagpur territories were interchanged between them for better coordination of their activities, and hence a full account of these activities involves a painstaking study of the materials in Government records offices in Calcutta, Madras and Nagpur, besides New Delhi.

Private papers of Governors-General, Bentinck, Auckland, Hardinge and Dalhousie, for example, are yet another source for the reconstruction of the history of the period when social reclamation of their subjects was for the rulers as important an object as military expansion of their empire and its administrative integration. Among officers on the spot, Campbell, Macpherson, Frye, Bannermann, Cadenhead, McViccar, McNeill, Hicks, Ricketts, Mills and Ousley, for example, some have left us, besides their official reports, their narratives, memoirs and diaries, and results of their researches on Kandh life and culture in contemporary learned journals and tracts. From all this emerges in intimate details the profile of a people of whom not much was known to the British government till the 1830s. These details provided the Government with the base on which its tribal policy in Orissa was structured.

The close involvement of Christian missionaries in this policy is evident from the proclaimed objectives of missionary societies and published accounts of individual missionaries.[4a] And finally, there are contemporary newspapers—*The Friend of India*—for example, which commended the Government's attempts at civilising the "savages" while cautioning it against rashness at times and condemning it for want of boldness at others.

But then, contemporary official and non-official accounts of female infanticide in the Ganjam hills are far less in volume and variety than those on human sacrifice which was viewed by officers as a far greater and far more gruesome evil. More widespread as the rite of human sacrifice was, it posed the Government a greater challenge than the practice of murdering female babies in the innermost recesses of a comparatively fewer Kandh homes. However, both the evils were tackled simultaneously, and the progressive decrease in their occurrence suggested the Government's success in tackling both the problems. And purely humanitarian consideration underlay the Government measures against them.[5]

As for the origin of female infanticide, the Kandh tradition had it that in ancient times two sisters, having failed to get husbands, got involved in incestuous relations with their first cousins—uncle's sons—and the resultant social disgrace drove them to suicide by drowning. The men blamed the girls for the social opprobrium suffered by the two families and decided to destroy their female children at birth itself as a precaution against the recurrence of such scandals in future.[6]

British officers quickly recognised the great hold of tradition on Kandh mind, but they also clearly saw the socio-economic compulsions underlying the tradition. The prejudices against women had a clear correlation with the endless disputes over property involved in the contraction of marriage relations and their dissolution. Custom obliged the Kandh bridegroom to pay bride price to his father-in-law which he had the right to get back if the wife deserted him. The girl's father in his turn was entitled to recover the amount from his daughter's latest husband. Since women could change their husbands at will and for limitless times, no Kandh with a married daughter could be sure as to the amount of property which he could call his own. If the wronged husband failed to get back the amount he had paid as the bride price, he could appeal to his wife's clan, and then the entire clan assumed the moral obligation to redress the man's grievance.[7] Personal disputes could then ramify into quarrels between clans, in the process deepening further the existing prejudice against women.

In Kandh society a woman's fidelity to just one man earned her not acclaim but taunts of other women, for a woman's social status in the infanticidal tracts was regulated by the number of men she had been able to entice, the intensity of intrigues she had been involved in, and the amount of property that had passed many hands following her many amorous escapades.[8] The only conventional restriction to her freedom to marry and remarry at will was her pregnancy and her having a child less than a year old. The mother could even take the child to her new home, the father, however, retaining his right to reclaim him when he had grown up.[9]

A wife's faithlessness—even an "ocular testimony of it"—did not bring on her the husband's wrath, for the Kandhs believed that "to strike a woman or even to insult her seriously would entail lasting disgrace upon a man's family".[10] As for the new husband, his erstwhile friendliness with the wronged husband would be restored as soon as the latter was paid the original bride price. Before the payment was made, a mock fight would be staged between the two men when "arms of courtesy"—and not bows and arrows—would be freely used; and then would follow, as a grand finale, a dinner of reconciliation for all clan members.[11]

For a woman remarriage was easy; easier still was elopement and living with the paramour. In fact, it was not the woman wishing to be a man's mistress but the man refusing to accept her as such who risked social damnation. In case of such refusal, mainly for poverty, the entire clan assumed the responsibility of somehow meeting the wish of the woman rather than suffer her jeers that the whole clan lacked in manliness.[12]

Conversely, for a man, his wife having deserted him, was a matter of great concern until he could find her replacement, which, however, was not easy, considering the scarcity of women in infanticidal tracts. In fact, the husband's natural desire to discipline his erring wife was checked by his fear of finding no woman at all to marry or even to live with—and such a situation was not deemed honourable in Kandh society.[13] Still, the existence of many unmarried Kandh men in Surada and other infanticidal tracts strongly suggested that they were too poor to pay the customary bride price and too wary to risk being involved in the endless disputes over claims and counter claims to property following their wives' unbridled promiscuity. Social obloquy of bachelorhood was painful indeed, but more fearful was the economic loss involved in disputes concerning women. No wonder, each matrimonial change caused so much trouble and vexation over property changing hands that for all but the rich patriarchs a married daughter was a veritable curse.[14] And to intensify this feeling was the parents' burdensome obligation to give their daughters some wedding gifts.[15]

Not just to display their "manliness", as the Kandhs said, but a more practical consideration motivated their preference for marrying girls of "foreign countries"[16]; such girls were far less expensive and far less likely to go back home at the slightest pretext and cause thereby inter-tribal clashes over demands for the refund of bride price. For the same reason the infanticidal Kandhs regarded it as "degrading" to give their daughters in marriage to men of "foreign countries".[17]

But then, the saving grace for the Government was the report that the Kandhs practising human sacrifice did not indulge in female infanticide, although they merrily killed women to propitiate the earth goddess for agricultural prosperity and for averting natural calamity.[18] The Kandhs believed that there lay an eternal conflict between the earth goddess of the "sacrificial" tribes and the Sun god of the infanticidal tribes who wanted his votaries to view women as a social evil and to bring up just as many of them as could be easily managed. And then, in some tracts there was another belief: female babies killed increased the prospects of more male births.[19]

No wonder, there were many tracts where no life of a female baby was spared except when a woman's first child was a girl or when the head of a clan or its branch wished to forge relations with a particular family by marriage. British officers saw not a single female child in some villages having over one hundred homes.[20]

The Government was determined to abolish female infanticide from the Kandh tracts, but were not sure enough of how to do it. For it was not just the prevention of a crime, but it involved changing the very mental frame of the tribals, their social outlook and their value system itself. Recourse to law was of little avail, for the Government's experience in Gujrat and Rajputana infanticidal tracts strongly suggested that the evidence needed for conviction was impossible to procure, the men attributing the death of female babies to disease and general poverty.[21] Besides, banning the practice by force would only drive it further from detection.

In fact, the men had to be convinced of the moral iniquity of the practice, not just threatened to give it up as a crime punishable by law. They should be made to realise that killing one's own offsprings was a morally outrageous act, not just a legally cognisable offence.

Moral suasion, and not coercion, was the approach needed; also patience and forbearance on the part of local officers apart from their courage and determination. The hold of tradition on the Kandh mind had to be loosened first, for the unhindered currency of the practice through the ages was viewed by them as the main justification for its continuance. The Kandhs found no criminality whatever in the practice because, as they said to British officers, their forefathers had found none either.

The Kandhs had to be made to see the practical benefit of rearing their female children, and this some British officers, particularly Macpherson, sought to do by emphasising the cause and effect relationship between the scarcity of women due to infanticide, the increasing bride price during their marriage, the loose marriage ties, the laxity in women's morals, and the endless disputes in Kandh society concerning women.[22] Macpherson also tried to gradually weaken the customary authority of tribal leaders to settle financial disputes and to induce the tribesmen to seek British officers' intercession either directly or through their trusted agents. The Government was determined to prevent the tribal propensity to make sanguinary settlement of most disputes. Macpherson strongly believed that justice humanised would secure stability in Kandh society, accustomed to endemic violence.[23]

The Government's first step was to establish contact with the Kandhs and keep up communication with them as a means of widening their mental horizon. British officers undertook regular tours in tribal tracts and even stayed in forest bungalows for months, thus narrowing the communication gap between the tribals and the Government. Over the years, the tribals overcame their fear of white officers and their distrust of the Indian subordinate staff of the Government; they became increasingly inquisitive of white officers and some became even gradually attached to them. British officers' earlier prejudice against the "savages" gradually wore off; they developed an understanding and sympathy for the tribals; for some traits of tribal character the officers made even very appreciative remarks.[24]

The officers' ignorance of the Kandh language was no handicap, for the local Oriya elite, an integral constituent of the tribal socio-political structure, were pressed into service as agents of the Government to execute its tribal policy.[25] The Oriya hill zamindars and their underlings, were tempted with rewards for helping the Government in the social reclamation of the tribals. The fact that the Oriyas living in Kandh tracts did not kill their girls was a guarantee that they would make no common cause with the infanticidal Kandhs. This was in welcome contrast to the situation in the "sacrificial" Kandh tracts where the local Oriya elite not only practised human sacrifice[26] at times but even sought to promote their political interests by supporting some local Kandh resistance to the Government's measures against the practice.[27]

British officers camping in infanticidal tracts insisted on taking the head count of female children, local chiefs being held responsible for any glaring disproportion between the male and female children; rewards were given to those who reared girls and punishment to those who killed them; it was brought home to the Kandhs that the Government was both earnest and determined to implement its policy.

Macpherson tried another—a more novel—experiment : to give the women rescued from sacrificial tracts in marriage to Kandh men of the infanticidal tracts (who could not marry for their inability to pay bride price), Government officers serving as foster guardians of the brides. No contract on bride price was executed before such marriages, but the Government met marriage expenses including customary gifts to the brides. Thus, some Kandh men, too poor to marry in their own tracts, now got wives, and so did some influential Kandh chiefs as a distinct mark of the Government's favour. [28] They would serve as conduits of the Government's influence in Kandh tracts.

By such "quasi-family" relations with the Kandhs, Macpherson hoped to extend and intensify the Government's influence in the region; the new wives had to be treated by their husbands as Government wards whose female babies must be reared, not killed.

The success of Macpherson's measures was reported by Cadenhead, who found after some years the Kandh ideas regarding infanticide having undergone a great modification:

> They have perceived the force and truth of his arguments, admit the futility of the practice, and deeply feel the imputations on their manhood involved in the continuance under the conditional religious sanction adduced by them while the rest of mankind do not require to resort to it.[29]

The fact that not a single girl had been killed in the two tracts of

Pendakhol and Digi since Macpherson had left Ganjam,[30] and that he had been able to save many girls' life in Bori and Goldi was indeed a heartening development in just a few months after Macpherson had adopted his measures.[31]

This, however, was rather an over-sanguine view. John Campbell, who had a longer experience of working in Kandh tracts than either Macpherson or Cadenhead, doubted much of their assertions. For example, unlike Macpherson, Cambell reported that female infanticide was not wholly unknown among the Kandhs who observed the rite of human sacrifice; the latter admitted to him of having occasionally killed their new-born female babies.[32] Even the girls, whose marriages with the infanticidal Kandhs had been solemnised by British officers, were found to have at times killed their female babies soon after their birth. Even these "foster children of the Government" on whom Macphersen had pinned a great hope, had ultimately succumbed to the compelling force of local tradition; conformity to the age-old custom secured for them social support while continued deference to the Government's wish carried the risk of social rejection.

Of the success of the measures of Macpherson, Campbell was not very optimistic either; he even strongly doubted both the truth and worth of Macpherson's claims. Campbell suspected that Macpherson's reports were drawn not on any first hand information collected by British officers, but on that supplied by their Indian subordinate staff; the latter's reports were "utterly unfounded and undeserving of confidence." The reported change in the Kandh mind, on which Macpherson and Cadenhead waxed so eloquent, was, in Campbell's view, "too much and too rapid to be credible."[33]

Campbell found no basis whatever for Macpherson's contention that Kandh women in general wielded "exceedingly great" influence in society and enjoyed a high status in it. [34] Except in the infanticidal tracts, Campbell found women's social position in all tribal tracts of Ganjam no different from anywhere else. They exercised no influence over men, took no part in communal deliberations, and their employment in hill tracts was "of the most menial description; they were the same "drudge and the slave of man", as anywhere else in India.[35]

Rather women's position in Kandh society was determined by their number in the local population. The lesser the number, the more their economic worth, and greater the scope for social instability following disputes to determine the worth. Thus, tracts with many women living in them had lesser problems over heavy bride price and lesser disputes over who paid the price and who recovered it from loss; in these tracts women changed their men in or out of wedlock as freely as men changing their numerous mistresses.[36] In some other tracts, however, concubinage was highly disgraceful for a woman, and to forestall the disgrace, local men killed female babies.[37]

All in all, Campbell's reports struck a far more realistic tone than Macpherson's. Female infanticide in Ganjam Kandh tracts was indeed a "very perplexing and difficult question"; the "gigantic plague" did not have as easy a remedy as Macpherson had led the Government to hope for. "The lamentable amount of deep-rooted superstition, pride, prejudice and poverty" which underlay the practice would require years of patience and perseverance on the part of Government officers to eradicate it; and the more so because the communication system in Ganjam hill areas was extremely difficult and the climate very unhealthy.[38]

Campbell's policy was a blend of moderation an resolution. In his scheme of things material development of the Kandh tracts and moral elevation of the Kandh mind constituted an integral process. Roads, markets and improved methods of cultivation were as important as schools and the scope provided to the tribals for closer and enduring contact with the non-tribal world. Campbell worked indefatigably for years, now hopeful and then frustrated, his missionary spirit alive nevertheless. The increasing number of female children gladdened him while his failure to register the names of parents of female wards caused him disappointment.[39] More frequent tours in the tracts, closer scrutiny of female babies and more stringent engagements extracted from Kandh chiefs to save girls were the steps he took. Not that he had any great faith in the efficacy of the engagements, but in the existing circumstances he could only hope that the commitment of Kandh chiefs would bind all the people who owed them customary allegiance. He knew that the men had an unreliable nature—sometimes "stolid, apathetic and listless", and at others "excited, passionate and restless"[40]—very different from what Macpherson had represented them to be.[41] Such men needed to be constantly watched and their apparent change of heart closely monitored, for:

> conviction may be professed, but in a little time old thoughts and old habits gain the ascendancy, and conversion is as far off as over.[42]

Nevertheless, Campbell was hopeful of raising a new generation of Kandhs in whose mind tradition would have a secondary place compared to the temptation of Government's favour as a means of personal advancement. He believed that the Kandhs "were not insensible either to the advantages which flow from the friendship of the *sarkar* and will not willingly forego them."[43]

Campbell coaxed mothers to bring him their daughters for physical verification of their number, and as inducement gave them coloured cloth and glass beads which they highly prized.[44] The fairs, markets and roads widened the economic frontier of the tribal tracts while schools where Oriya and Kandh children studied together wrought a slow moral development in the latter. In 1854, just before leaving Ganjam, Campbell could happily find in the infanticidal tracts of Surada and Chinakimedy many female children where just five years ago very few, if any, girls could be seen.[45]

Campbell's policy of "caution, admonition and encouragement" was continued by his successors, Macdonald, McViccar and McNeill. Macdonald was glad seeing the Kandhs' eagerness to get their disputes settled by British officers and the increasing traffic of the tribals to the markets and fairs set up by Campbell.[46] McViccar sought to tighten the "local control" on the infanticidal tracts to prevent any glaring disproportion between the male and female children there. In May 1855 he could report to the Government that he had counted 907 male and 434 female children in a population of 1415 male adults and 998 female adults.[47]

McNeill, the last Agent in the Hill tracts of Orissa, visited Jeypur, an extensive zamindary close to Ganjam, where in hilly tracts both male and female infanticide were prevalent to a very considerable extent. Jeypur Kandhs were "comparatively civilised and well off," but local astrologers, mostly Oriyas, exploited the "credulity and superstition" of the tribals to induce them to kill children who were supposed to bring evil to the family, the clan or the community. McNeill paraded some infanticidal Kandhs in irons at market places in Surada so that the local men could have "an ocular proof" of the Government's wrath.[48]

McNeill shared both Campbell's confidence and disappointment. The results of his sample survey of some tracts pleased him : in 1859-60, he found as many as 976 girls aged six and below and 1199 boys of the same age at places where in 1854-55, he had seen only 870 girls and 1815 boys; the female children population had increased by 80 per cent in just six years. But then, he found evidence of female infanticide not being wholly unknown even in the sacrificing Kandh tracts of upper Ghumsur where the hold of the Government on local Kandhs was the strongest. A Kandh woman killed her twin daughters believing that a great calamity would befall her family if she reared them. But then, there was also the sight of many local Kandhs parading their wives before McNeill to convince him that they had given up the practice of female infanticide.[49]

The Orissa Hill Agency was wound up in 1861, the Government complementing itself on having set in motion a force with which to change the Kandh society. By then, female infanticide may not have been abolished altogether, but the Government's policy had indeed caused a dent to the practice which had been current for centuries. McNeill for himself had no doubt whatever that inspite of the claims of Kandh *sardars* of having uprooted the tradition, "the disproportion of the sexes too plainly proves that in many districts this great evil still obtained to a great extent".[50] There were many still unvisited and indeed impassable tribal tracts; it was impossible to take correct census of the local population to establish the ratio of females to the males there; above all, the people involved were far too many for a few British officers to either coerce or conciliate in order to implement the policy of humanising the tribals.

The local elite, both Kandh *sardars* and Oriya zamindars and their underlings, had a limited accountability for the success of the Government's scheme; unlike in the infanticidal tracts of Kutch and Kathiawar, for instance, the Government could not impose fines on those who disobeyed its orders. Nor did the Government raise a fund in the Kandh tracts, as it had done in Kathiawar and Kutch again,[51] as the source of bride price to be paid to indigent parents for the marriage of their daughters. The Government's interest in Ganjam Kandh tracts was far too limited to impel it to set up such a fund, let alone the local elite being called upon to contribute to it. And above all, from most of these tracts the Government realised no land revenue at all.

Indeed, the achievements of the Government could be measured not so much by the actual number of female children that it could save, but by the idea it implanted in the Kandh mind that no tradition, however old and deep rooted, was beyond the interference of the Government; and it is this idea which more than anything else helped make the British tribal policy in Orissa a gradual success. At least "the germs of an ultimate civilisation have been planted in the country" which enabled the Government to confidently hope "that the advance of the population towards a higher social condition will be in an accelerated ratio of progress".[52] In this hope lay the main motivation of the British policy in Ganjam tribal tracts in later years.

Notes & References

1. *Selections from the Records of the Madras Government No. XXIV of 1856: Russell's Reports on the Disturbances in Parlakimedy, Vizagapatnam and Goomsoor in 1832-36,* 2 Vols. (Madras, 1856).
2. See HRPO, *op. cit.* and *Reports of the Meriah Agents (Ganjam) from 1837-1861* (Madras, 1885).
3. *Ibid.*
4. There was a large Kandh population in Daspalla and Boud, two tributary states under Bengal, Karonde (Kalahandi) and Bastar, tributary states under the Bhonsles of Nagpur, and in the tributary states of Sonpur, Patna and Bamra under the South-West Frontier Agency.

4a. In the *Calcutta Christian Observer,* the *Missionary Herald* and the *Oriental Baptist* there are numerous references to the involvement of missionaries in the social redemption project in Kandh tracts. S. Pearce Carey, *op. cit.* Barbara M. Boal, *The Church in the Kond Hills* (1963). Dasarathi Swaro, *op. cit.*, pp. 128-60.

5. Barbara M. Boal, 1982, *op cit.*, pp. 66-70. Female infanticide prevailed in Surada, Goradah and Chinnakimedy zamindaries which covered an area of 2,400 Square miles with a population of 60,000. Every year, on an average 1,200 to 1,500 girls were killed in these tracts. HRPO, *op. cit.*, p. 66.
6. J. Campbell to Govt., 11 Jan. 1849, HP, 3 Feb. 1849, No. 20.
7. *Reports of the Meriah Agents, op. cit.,* p. 11 : Report of Captain Macpherson to the Agent to the Governor of Madras in Ganjam, 24 Apr. 1842
8. *Ibid.,* pp. 11-2. Macpherson to R.A. Bannerman, Agent in Ganjam, 24 Apr. 1842 in *Selections from the Old Records of the Ganjam Collectorate* (Chatrapur, 1936), *p. 23* (hereafter SRGC).
9. *Ibid.* p. 24.
10. *Ibid.*
11. *Ibid.*
12. *Ibid.*
13. *Ibid.*

14 BJCP, 19 Jun 1843, No. 100 : Macpherson to Bannerman, 31 May 1843.

15. *Ibid.*

16 *Narrative by Major General John Campbell of his operations in the hill tracts of Orissa for the suppression of human sacrifice and female infanticide* (London, 1861), p. 80.

17. HRPO, p. 108 : Campbell to Govt., 19 Aug. 1848.
18. *Ibid.* p. 2
19. *Ibid.*, pp. 66-67 : Macpherson to Govt., 10 July 1844.
20. *Ibid.*, SRGC, p. 23 : Macpherson's Report, 24 Apr. 1842.
21. Lalita Panigrahi, *British Social Policy and Female Infanticide in India (*New Delhi, 1972), p. 41.
22. *The Calcutta Review,* Vol. X (July-Dec. 1848), pp. 319-20.
23. S. C. Macpherson's *Report Upon the Khonds of the Districts of Ganjam and Cuttack* (Madras, 1863), pp. 84-5.
24. *Reports of the Meriah Agents (Ganjam) op. cit.,* pp. 1-36.
25. Campbell, *Narrative, op. cit.,* pp. 258-61.
26. The report of Campbell and Macpherson contain many references to the Oriya chiefs and zamindars in Ganjam tribal tracts observing the rite of human sacrifice to appease the gods or avert their wrath.
27. For example, Chakra Bissoyi of Ghumsur, who wanted the restoration of the Bhanja dynasty's rule on Ghumsur, incited the local Kandhs to rise against the British government which had ended the rule and taken cver the estate. He assured the Kandhs that with the Bhanjas restored to power, human sacrifice, banned by the British, would be resumed. This was in 1846-7. Chakra Bissoyi again sought to create ill-feelings between the Kandhs and the British government in 1855-6, offering them the same temptation. Madras Revenue Consultations, Jan-Feb. 1847: Letters of Macpherson, Bannerman and Cadenhead. P. Mukherjee, *History of Orissa* (Utkal, University, 1964), pp. 197-208. Maltby, *op. cit.,* p. 157.
28. William Macpherson, *Memorials, op. cit.,* pp. 223-5.
29. *Reports of the Meriah Agents (Ganjam), op. cit.,* p. 21 : J. Cadenhead to Acting Agent, Ganjam, 17 Mar. 1845.
30. *Ibid.*
31 *Ibid.*
32. HRPO, p. 134 : Campbell to Govt., 9 Feb. 1854.
33. *Home Department* (Public) Proceedings, NAI (hereafter HP), 31 Mar. 1849, No. 15 : Campbell to Govt., 17 Mar. 1849.
34. *Ibid.* Macpherson reported that the Kandhs found their women's aid indispensable in battles as also during peace making; they greatly influenced the decisions of Kandh chiefs. William Macpherson, *op. cit.,* p. 132.
35. HP, 31 Mar. 1849, No. 15 : Campbell to Govt., 17 Mar. 1849.
36. *Report of Meriah Agents (Ganjam), op. cit.,* p. 12 : Macpherson to Govt., 24 Apr. 1842.

37. *Ibid.* It must be remembered that Campbell bore grudges against Macpherson, and sought to belittle his achievements. Boal, 1982, p. 74.
38. HP, 2 Sept. 1848, No. 59: Campbell to Govt., 19 Aug. 1848; 31 Mar. 1849: No. 15: Campbell to Govt., 17 Mar. 1849.
39. *Ibid.* Campbell reported " ... the people fled in great alarm, asserting that they were sure to die, if I persisted in my design of numbering them."
40. Campbell, *A Personal Narrative, op. cit.,* p. 252.
41. Macpherson found the Kandhs possessing "a clear and vigorous intellect ... slow of deliberation, but prompt to act"; besides, they had a "passionate love of liberty". See his *Report Upon the Khonds, op. cit.,* pp. 52, 59. Also see William Macpherson, *op. cit.,* p. 179.
42 HP, 31 March 1849, No. 15 : Campbell to Govt., 17 Mar. 1849.
43. *Ibid.*
44. HRPO, Campbell to Govt., 13 Apr. 1853.
45. *Ibid.*
46. *Report of Meriah Agents (Ganjam), op. cit.* p. 52, R. M. Macdonald, Asst. Agent, to Acting Agent, Ganjam, 31 Jan. 1855, p. 52.
47. *Ibid.* p. 58, McVicaar to Govt, 21 May 1855.
48. *Ibid.*, p. 67, McNeill to Govt., 12 May 1857; p. 69, McNeill to Govt., 28 Jan. 1858.
49. *Ibid.*, p. 69-76, McNeill to Govt., 16 Apr., 14 May, 27 May 1859.
50. *Ibid.*, p. 79, McNeill to Govt., 26 May 1861.
51. Panigrahi, *op. cit.*, pp. 41, 51. A. Das, Female Infanticide in Western India During Nineteenth Century (Unpublished M. Phil dissertation, University of Bombay, 1988), pp. 64-5, 70, 72-4.
52. HRPO, P. 134 : Despatch from the Court of Directors to Governor-General, 14 June 1854.

6

Bonded Labour in the Ganjam Agency : Dichotomy in British Tribal Policy

An important problem faced by the British administrators of the Ganjam Agency was the developing conflict between the concept of a protective and paternalistic rule over the local aboriginal people and the compulsions of administrative needs which made the concept increasingly untenable. An illustration of this problem could be provided by the British government's attitude to the institution of bonded labour in the Agency.

Bonded labour was called in official despatches *vetti,* a corruption of the Oriya word, *bethi.* The tribesmen, mainly Kandhs and Savaras, had to render unpaid service to the local Oriya elite, called *muthadars* or village headmen, whose official designation at some places was *patro* and at others *bissoyi.* Each village, as the unit of tribal administration, had to furnish a contingent of labourers to the local *patro* or *bissoyi* for agricultural operations, such as sowing, weeding and reaping, as also for thatching houses and procuring fodder from forests. The Oriya elite also received from local tribesmen *mamuls* or free gifts of fruits and vegetables, fowls and goats, oil, salt, honey, rice, herbs and other forest products for their own consumption and as offerings to village deities.

Even the Oriya elite's retainers, the *naiks* and *paiks,* the hereditary militia, to maintain local law and order, received this unpaid service and free gifts. The items of the *mamuls* and their quantity, the time and occasion of their payment were all fixed and unalterable, and this was well known to both the givers and receivers. Such too was the case with the *vetti.*[1] The likely proneness of the recipients to demand more free service or free gifts than customary was balanced by their fear of possible resistance by the tribesmen.

Together, the *vetti* and *mamul* formed a part of the institutional base of the feudalistic structure of tribal life. For the Oriya elite they were a means of exercising control over the tribesmen; for the latter they were a symbol of loyalty to the elite. The two institutions had the sanction of no written law or regulation; custom and usage alone had guaranteed their persistence through the ages. Peace in Ganjam tribal tracts had depended not inconsiderably on the tribesmen's acceptance of their customary obligation to the Oriya *muthadars,* and the latter's general desistance from extortion.

Change came in the wake of the British rule with "civilising mission" as its declared aim in the wild tract, accustomed for ages to *laissez faire* as the practical principle of administration. The traditional pattern of relations between different segments of tribal society now tended to change due partly to the policy of the new rulers and partly to the concatenation of circumstances, the result of forces released by the new administration. With the many appurtenances of a settled administration, such as the courts, the police, roads and postal communication, markets and trade centres, medical and educational establishments, there were now far better means of maintaining law and order; also much larger scope for influencing the tribal mind. All this had an impact on the institution of *vetti.*

Early Agency officers saw nothing iniquitous in this institution; it was rather useful to administration. It served to maintain the traditional hold of the Oriya *muthadars* on the tribals, the hold which the British, like all earlier rulers, found indispensable for consolidating their rule in tribal tracts and implementing their policies there. The British government's policy was to attach the *muthadars* to itself by increasing their stakes in the new administration and by progressively coordinating their interests with its own.

The Oriya *patros, bissoyis* and *paiks* functioned as the principal agency of the British administration in tribal tracts of Ganjam. With the resultant increase in powers, the Oriya elite's proneness to abuse their traditional authority on the tribals increased as well.[2] Used by the Government as agents of change in tribal life, they soon turned out to be the main agency of local oppression.

The best example of this tendency lay in their forcing the Kandhs and Savaras to render unpaid labour for the construction and maintenance of roads and buildings in tribal tracts—a task which the Government entrusted to the Oriya elite. For the Government roads were a military necessity as also the means of opening up the wild tracts for trade and commerce; roads were also looked upon as a means of disseminating "the civilising influence of a benevolent administration."

But then, Agency officers found the execution and maintenance of civil works in the hilly and unhealthy tracts by engaging labourers brought from the plains both a difficult and expensive undertaking. For the works the Government used to make a liberal monthly grant to Agency officers who, in their turn, depended on their head clerks for getting *coolies* from the plains, paying them wages and supervising their work. Often the clerks cooked up the accounts and embezzled public money. The *coolies* fell sick in the inhospitable tracts which delayed the works.[3]

In such circumstances, at places influential and popular Agency officers got some works done by engaging tribal labour, paying the men a very nominal wage and thus saving a lot of Government money. At some other places *patros* and *bissoyis* were given the responsibility, and they got the works executed by *vetti.* These works, particularly the roads, proved far more economical and far more durable than those executed by *coolies* brought from the plains.[4] Agency officers hoped that such a practice of employing tribal labour for Government works would create in the local men an economic stake; the country opened up by roads would soon turn the "semi-barbarous and excitable population" into "peaceable and ordinary ryots".[5]

Thus the practice took root, but as yet without any formal Government sanction. In 1875, the Acting Agent, R. Davidson, made a strong plea for the sanction. He criticised the existing rules for executing the Agency civil works which had cost the Government over the years a considerable amount of money,[6] the works having been done by *coolies* of the plains in a most "perfunctory and unsystematic way", many roads having just been washed away in the rains. Davidson pressed for an "entire change in the system" and for the formal adoption of the policy of getting the works done by the Oriya elite—a practice which had been found both effective and economical. Even the small wages given to tribal labourers would improve their economic condition besides attaching them closer to Government.[7]

The Government was impressed, but all that it did was to acquiesce in the practice, not give it even now any formal official sanction. The Acting Agent's arguments were no doubt weighty, but there lurked a nagging fear : the Oriya elite would misuse their new responsibility and power to further oppress the tribals.

To such a possibility, Lord Napier, the Governor of Madras,[8] had himself drawn pointed attention in 1866 when dealing with a tribal outbreak in parts of the Agency. Napier had attributed the disturbance to tribal resistance to the increasing oppression of the Oriya elite who demanded unpaid labour for Agency civil works and more gifts from the tribals as their customary *mamul.* Napier had been little impressed by official reports about large number of tribals having cheerfully worked on roads though paid a very small wage. He had dismissed the reports of both the Inspector-General of Police and the Acting Agent as being without the "stamp of completeness, reflection and impartiality". The Governor was convinced that the Agency administration was defective and that the tribal grievances were just.[9]

All this weighed with the Government when considering Davidson's proposal. It could not ignore the cost factor involved in the Agency civil works any more than it could formally allow the Oriya elite to force the tribals to render unpaid service to execute the works. In such circumstances, the Government adopted what was patently an ambivalent attitude to the issue. It appreciated the "most excellent work done by the Kandhs through the influence of the *patros",* and that so cheaply; but it refused to make such service obligatory for the Kandhs, for they were primarily farmers and hunters and so "*coolie* labour was uncongenial to their disposition." The Government would not officially ban the *vetti* for getting its civil works executed, but local officers were asked to observe "cautious discretion" in allowing its wide practice lest the *patros* and *bissoyis* stretched their traditional right to get free service by the tribals much too far.[10] The Government's policy was to avoid interference with the traditional right of the Oriya elite until its misuse set off a violent tribal reaction.

The Government's ambivalence made the practice of its civil works done by tribal *vetti* an established one; by the turn of the 19th century the Oriya elite had extended the practice widely, in the process making the most of it to their own advantage. Agency officers advanced money to *patros* and *bissoyis* to employ tribal labour for road works, for thatching Government forest bungalows, for carrying officers' luggages and for supplying raw materials for civil works. The *patros* and *bissoyis* assigned the work housewise, and not to particular individuals. Thus, particular villages were made responsible for particular items of work year after year. Unlike the *coolies* of the plains, tribal labourers did not work at any particular and fixed time of the day nor even regularly for some days; and so muster roll of such labourers could not be maintained nor was it possible to pay them daily wages at a fixed rate based on the quantum of work they did each day.[11]

Under such circumstances, the Oriya *muthadars* could easily "overtask and underpay the tribal labourers." Very often they did not make any payment at all, insisting on unpaid service as the customary tribal obligation. The subordinate staff of the Agency were hand in glove with the *patros* and *bissoyis* in exploiting the Kandhs and Savaras; they got the thumb impression of the ignorant and simple tribal labourers on official papers to show that the men had received their due while in fact a far lesser amount had actually been paid to them. Police constables got rice and other local products from the tribals very cheaply and sold them in the plains at a much higher price.[12] Oriya *muthadars* acted as middlemen in such transactions.

Roads brought economic mobility to Agency tracts, and the Government's "civilising" measures implemented through the Oriya elite added a new dimension to the *vetti* issue. *Patros* and *bissoyis* helped in the establishment and maintenance of markets, in the growth of import and export trade, and in the development of the money economy in tribal tracts. In the process they improved their economic position; they now needed more *vetti* for the new farm lands they acquired and for the new houses they built. Alongside, the volume and variety of the *mamuls* they extracted from the tribals kept increasing too.[13]

Greater was the tribal misery when the Government launched upon a policy of conservation of forests, preventing the tribals from acquiring new forest lands for cultivation. The men had no knowledge of settled and intensive cultivation of definite tracts, slash and burn, locally called *podu,* being the traditional mode of agriculture. The Government declared some forests as reserved where *podu* was banned.[14] The Oriya elite helped the Government in the operation of forest laws and realisation of forest revenue through the sale and export of timber, in particular.[15] In consequence, tribesmen found it harder to give the Oriya elite the customary *mamul* in the form of forest products, such as honey and herbs; they had to pay money instead or do more vetti in lieu of money.

Tribal economic plight was graver following progressive loss of their land to rapacious Oriya usurers who took the fullest advantage of the honesty, innocence and gullibility of the Kandhs and Savaras.[16] The tribals never got back their lands mortgaged to the usurers even after they had cleared their debts together with interest. Sometimes the tribals had to do *vetti* to clear the debts incurred by their forbears many decades ago.[16a]

Agency officers' reports clearly established the correlation between the increasing Government civil works, mainly roads, the widening responsibility and powers of the *patros* and *bissoyis,* their tendency to exact more *vetti* and *mamul* than customary and simmering tribal discontent.[17] To stem the worsening relations between the Oriya elite and the tribesmen, the Government had to fix a definite limit to the former's claims and the latter's obligations; hence a *mutha*-wise schedule of *mamul* and *vetti* was compiled from time to time, taking into consideration both local conventions and changing economic conditions.[18] At places *patros* and *bissoyis* were required to give receipts to the tribal people as written acknowledgement of free service and gifts. An act was passed in 1917 to prevent land alienation to non-tribal immigrants to Agency tracts. The bissoyis of Parlakhemundi were required to give *batta* to the Savaras when they did manual service to them.

The Government's general policy was to check any wanton exploitation of the tribals by the Oriya elite while safeguarding the latter's accustomed position in the Agency. It would punish both the recalcitrant Kandhs and Savaras as well as extortionate *patros, bissoyis* and *paiks*. As for *vetti,* the Government was aware of the possibility of the "unrestricted development of this system to unlimited oppression" and the resultant discontent in the tribal people,[19] but as long as it did not escalate into a widespread and general disturbance, it chose not to interfere with the system.

With the years more and more tribal tracts were opened up, and alongside the tribal mind too, the result of easier contact with the people of the plains and more frequent interaction with them as traders and employees of the Government. New wants and new tastes developed among the tribals; they now craved for articles imported from the plains, such as soap, fine mill cloth, tea, hair oil and cigarette.[20] Education and Christian evangelical activity[21] accelerated this process of change in tribal life.

Some tribals were no longer as docile and acquiescent as before; they developed a spirit of resistance to measures harmful to their interests. Their erstwhile submissiveness to *muthadars* tended to change into occasional defiance,[22] the result of the Government's steps to protect them from overt exploitation and the increasing scope of redressal of their grievances by Agency officers who could now reach the hitherto inaccessible tracts by roads built by the tribals themselves.

Savara demand for more lands for *podu* cultivation kept pace with the extension of Government reserved forests and their inability to meet the Oriya elite's demand for more free gifts. In 1922, the Savara defiance of forest laws led to a widespread outbreak in the Parlakhemundi Agency area where the *bissoyi's* demand for *mamuls* had assumed "extravagant proportions."[23] The disturbance was no doubt quelled but not before the Government was obliged to allow ten acres of *podu* land to each Savara house which led to the disafforestation of 15,800 acres of land by the next decade.[24]

With their new awareness and extended experiences, the tribals would no longer view their traditional institutions as before; this was most evident in their growing reluctance to do *vetti* and give *mamul.* The new mood found articulation in the panas mostly, traditionally the shrewdest element in tribal society. Originally immigrant pariahs from the foothills and plains, the panas, after long habitation in Agency tracts, had become an integral part of tribal society socio-economic life.[25] As petty traders, they constituted the traditional economic link between the hills and the plains, the tribals and non-triabls. Like the Kandhs and Savaras, they too had the customary obligation to the Oriya elite in the form of rendering free service and giving free gifts.

At places the panas embraced Christianity and, under the missionary influence and some education, became not only conscious but assertive of their rights. They would not do *vetti* either for the Government or for local *patros* and *bissoyis*, contending that their changed social status after conversion to Christianity should free them from their traditional obligation.[26] They would rather prefer being fined for dereliction of their customary duty to the Oriya elite than be forced to work for them or for the Government with little or no payment. Both the Oriya *muthadars* and Government officers viewed the Christian panas as the most troublesome element in the Ganjam Agency whose defiant attitude seemed to influence the tribals too. The Savaras of Parlakhemundi, for example, took the cue soon, refusing to do *vetti* and give *mamul.* Some of them would rather make payment to the *muthadar* than do unpaid service to him; some even engaged lawyers to move the court.[27]

In such circumstances the Government had to decide whether to dispense with *vetti* altogether when the times were evidently changing. The issue became an urgent one when the expanding civil works in tribal tracts needed more cheap labour for their execution. There was another consideration: any impairment of the traditional authority of the local Oriya elite following the abolition of the *vetti* system, would add to the responsibility of Government officers. In such a situation the

Government chose to defer a final decision in the matter; all that it did was to institute an enquiry into the working of the *vetti* system to prevent any large scale exploitation of the tribals by the *muthadars*. Such an enquiry was also needed to convince the Government that *vetti* was not exactly the same as forced labour which the International Labour Organisation had been very strongly condemning.

The enquiry established that the system of *vetti* as prevalent in the Ganjam Agency had a threefold character : (i) service for the execution and maintenance of Agency civil works which provided for a very nominal payment to the labourers, (ii) service for the transport of Government and other luggages at a prescribed low rate, and (iii) service by the tribals as a part of their traditional obligation to *muthadars,* to other village officials (*naik* and *paiks,* for example) and to village deities looked after by the local Oriya elite. The last kind of service alone had the sanction of tribal custom and tradition and had been officially recognised by the Government; the two others had just been co-eval with the development of the Agency administration which had acquiesced in their persistence due to their utility to the administration itself.[28]

The enquiry also established the great abuse of *vetti* by the Oriya elite whom the Government had made responsible for the execution and maintenance of Agency civil works.[29] The abuse of this traditional institution had of late increased very much when the needs of the Agency administration had increased and along with it its dependence on the Oriya elite. Agency officers had themselves often compelled the tribals to do *vetti* on the mistaken idea that the Government had the right to demand cheap labour from them because they paid no land tax whatever, and because the roads they built benefited them.[30] Even those tribesmen who served as Government forest guards and had either little time to do *vetti* or disliked it as degrading, were not spared; Agency officers insisted that the men provide substitutes to do *vetti.* The Savaras of Ramgiri-Udaygiri complained that even Government officers demanded *vetti* service on personal account.[31]

The tyranny of the *patros* and *bissoyis* had increased in direct proportion to the expansion of Agency civil works in recent years; the economic condition of the tribals had worsened while the Agency administration budget recorded a consistant surplus.[32] What aggravated the situation was that the Government's demand for cheap tribal labour was the greatest during the winter months when local men worked in their fields. The resultant tribal discontent intensified with the unabated loss of land to Oriya immigrants despite the law intended to protect tribal interests. The tribals, particularly of the hills, were mostly ignorant of the provisions of the 1917 Act; fearful of Oriya money lenders, who fleeced them, they could not even move the Government for protection; they were "honest, unsophisticated and regarded their debt as one of honour:.[33] The subordinate staff of the Agency did not enforce the Act as strongly as could make it serve the intended purpose. After the enquiry, the Ganjam Agency office admitted :

> Except the custom, the agency people are under no statutory obligation to render *vetti* service, and it cannot be enforced without extraordinary trouble and expense in case of general refusal.[34]

What complicated the situation further was the rivalry between the Public Works Department and the Revenue Department for executing the Agency civil works. The P.W.D. contended that it had the requisite expertise to do the job, while the Revenue Department claimed long experience of managing the tribals which alone had enabled the Government to get its civil works in tribal tracts done and maintained since the very establishment of the tribal administration in Ganjam. The Government then struck a compromise : arterial roads were entrusted to the P.W.D., while others were retained by the Revenue Department, the Agent's overall control of all the civil works in the tribal tracts remaining unchanged.[35] But then, the PWD paid the tribal labourers better wages than the Revenue Department did with the result that the latter found it hard to get labourers as cheaply as it was accustomed to under the *vetti* system;[36] all this was made known to the Government by Agency officers.

By the 1930s the situation had come to such a pass that the increasingly unpopular system could not be continued indefinitely while without it, the Agency civil works, now much extended, would cost the Government much more than it could afford, particularly when it derived no land revenue whatever from most of the Agency tracts.[37] To force the tribals to render unpaid, or meagrely paid, service was morally wrong because as one Agent himself admitted :

> There is no sanction of the theory that the hillmen hold their land on condition of doing *vetti* service, though the practice had grown up to expect them to perform such service for a low remuneration. Actually many who do *vetti* service . . . . no longer own land, having been dispossessed.[38]

Besides, it was "incompatible to the modern idea of civilisation."[39]

But then, to do away with the practice altogether was an impracticable proposition from the economic point of view; and this had been repeatedly brought to the knowledge of the Government by the Agency administration.

The Government's dilemma was clearly reflected in the annual Agency conferences where local officers expressed conflicting views regarding the *vetti* system. While there was general agreement that the tribals deserved sympathetic treatment, opinion was sharply divided on whether or not the system would be done away with immediately. With the impoverished tribes grumbling, the exactions of the *muthadars* increasing, and the Agency staff hard put to pacify the one and restrain the other, a section of officers would either give up the *vetti* system or pay the tribal labourers more wages to do the Government jobs willingly. They were confident that even with the resultant increased expenditure, the Revenue Department would be able to execute and maintain the Agency civil works far more cheaply than the PWD could by engaging *coolies* from the plains.[40]

However, this optimism was not shared by others for whom the continuance of the *vetti* system was but a necessary evil, having both an economic and political justification. Its abolition was, they feared, certain to undermine the accustomed hold of the Oriya elite on the awakening tribals, some of whom had lately been prosecuted for involvement in the Civil Disobedience Movement.[41] As A.R.C., Westlake, the Agent, put it:

> ... without *vetti* labour the administration of the agency would either break down or the Government would have to foot a surprisingly large bill. The abolition of compulsory labour is no doubt a necessary concomitant of the march of civilisation, but its abolition in the agency will, as the Special Assistant Agent, Chicacole, aptly remarks, leave civilisation with no roads to march on.[42]

Some officers suggested that the tribals and the panas be given the option of either doing *vetti* or commuting it for a fixed payment with which to secure substitutes to do their work.[43] The Agency conference of 1934 ended its deliberations on the *vetti* by concluding that

> the employment of *vetti* labour was still necessary to the limited extent that it is now employed and was justified by the absence of other forms of taxation.[44]

The officers sought comfort by observing that the *vetti* system in the Ganjam Agency was not as bad a form of servile labour as was prevalent—and that far more widely—in the Orissa princely states.[45]

Thus, local official opinion being far from unanimous, the Government's decision on the matter could just be as ambivalent as heretofore. While it was but natural for people "rising in the scale of civilisation" to grumble if not adequately paid for the service they rendered,[46] it was also very expensive to get the civil works executed by paying high wages to labourers in a tract from which the Government received little land revenue. There was also a moral question involved : in 1846, the Government had given the tribals an unequivocal promise to impose no land tax on them nor exact service labour.[47] Hence, while practically forcing the men to work for the Government and fobbing them off with a pittance, Agency officers had for long been actually breaking the pledge. It was indeed a difficult situation for the Government: it was as much convinced of the undesirability of abolishing the *vetti* system altogether as it was concerned over the effect of its continuance when the temper of the times was changing and the tribals were getting restive.

Hence, the utmost that the Government could do in such circumstances was to decide to pay more wages to those willing to work, and not to compel the unwilling ones.[48] The Government would now allow only the *patros* and *bissoyis* to claim *vetti,* not their retainers as hitherto.[49] The Government would provide alternative employment to those who demanded more land for *podu;* henceforth, officers would be more vigilant to prevent the rapacity of Oriya *muthadars* whose demand for *mamuls* and *vetti* was now adjusted to the existing economic condition of the tribals. The practice of Agency officers travelling on chairs slung along the back of tribal porters was stopped, for such a service was resented by the tribals as a "disgrace". For carrying Government luggages, higher rates were fixed. As an incentive to good work by the *muthadars,* it was suggested that they be presented with a piece of cloth on which their name would be inscribed, and that Savara *coolies* be offered cheroots and snuff, instead of money, as wages. The tribals were urged to demand from *patros* and *bissoyis* written acknowledgement of free service and free gifts to serve as a legal armour against further demands for such service and gifts in the near future.[50]

With all this, the *vetti* labour would not be as cheap as before. The problem now was how to meet the increased bill of Agency civil works. Agency officers were unanimous that the panas and Oriya immigrants, who had benefitted most from the Agency administration, should either pay land tax or render *vetti* service as they had done for years in the past but which they had been unwilling to do lately.[51] In fact, what the poor tribals grudged most was that while the Government pressed them hard for regular *vetti* service and even *mamul,* the Oriya immigrants and panas, economically far better off, were not treated as harshly.

But then, the Government could hardly overlook the fact that the panas had so long been recognised as a scheduled tribe,[52] and so, like other tribals, they too could not be asked to pay land tax without contravening the Government's own promise in 1846 not to do so. The panas and the Oriya immigrants living for years in the tribal tracts had in consequence been so much an integral part of the local tribal socio-economic life that no step towards them alone could be taken without affecting thereby the general tribal life itself. The issue was indeed very complicated, involving the adoption of a clear cut policy towards *vetti* and *mamul.* The Madras government chose to shelve the issue, for its rule over the Ganjam Agency was about to end, the tract being included in the projected new province of Orissa. And there the matter rested in 1936, the Madras government having left it to the new government of Orissa to tackle.[53]

In the hundred years of its rule over the Ganjam Agency, the Madras government was hard put to reconcile two conflicting considerations in dealing with the institution of *vetti* or bonded labour: the moral impropriety of its continuance in the changing circumstances, and the great economic loss and political risk involved in its desuetude. New socio-economic forces released by the British administration had their inevitable impact on the accustomed pattern of tribal life; the maintenance of this life, however desirable, proved increasingly difficult. Administrative necessity naturally called for some change in the existing official policy with a view to helping the tribal life develop in accordance with the prevalent concept of modernism while avoiding any direct conflict with the traditional mores of the life.

The ideals of a *laissez faire* and humane administration had to be accommodated with the principle of economic viability as the base of a modern and efficient administration. Paternalistic concern and care for the aboriginals was indeed a laudable idea till the colonial government did not have to pay too high a price for its implementation. The administration needed to be cost-effective, not just benevolent.

Notes and References

1. *Report of C. F. MacCartie on the bissoyis of Parlakhemundi,* 24 Nov. 1881. A Mounsey, *History of the Ganjam Maliahs* (Madras, 1884). M. D. Taylor, *Memorandum on the Ganjam Maliahs* (Reprint, Cuttack, 1949), p. 118.
2. Ganjam Collectorate Records (hereafter GC), Chatrapur, File No. R. Dis. 4197/1931 : Agent, Ganjam to Superintendent, Census Operations, 29 Jun. 1931. Madras Judicial Proceedings, Tamil Nadu Archives, Madras (hereafter MJP, 20 Mar. 1866, No. 142. Also Reports of Taylor, MacCartie and Mounsey, *op. cit.*
3. MJP, 6 Jan. 1876, No. 21 : R. Davidson, Acting Agent, Ganjam, to Madras Govt., 7 June 1875.
4. In 1865, more than 200 miles of road were constructed by tribal labour at a cost of only Rs. 3000, MJP, 23 Dec. 1865, No. 196.
5. *Ibid.* No. 194 : W. Robinson, Inspector General, Police, to Madras Govt., 17 July 1865.
6. Annually the Agent received from the Government Rs. 5,000 for new road construction, and Rs. 5,200 for the repair of old roads, which in 1874 was increased to Rs. 5,900. MJP, 18 Apr. 1874, No. 91.
7. MJP, 6 Jan 1876, No. 21, *op. cit.*
8. Napier was Governor of Madras in 1866-72.
9. MJP, 20 Mar. 1866, Nos. 142-46 : Report on Kutiya Khond Uprising. *Minutes Recorded by Lord Napier* (Madras, 1873), pp. 60-63. Over two hundred miles of road were constructed in less than four months. For details see below, pp.78-79, 82
10. MJP, 6 January 1876 : Govt. Order No. 14, 6 Jan. 1876.
11. GC., File No. 6756/1926 : Ganjam Agency Office Note on the evolution of the *vetti* system. Also *Ibid.*, File No. 1835/1934.
12. *Ibid.* GC, File No. 3519/1936; GC, Proceedings of the Special Asst. Agent, 8 Mar. 1880.
13. MJP, Govt. Order 26 January 1886, No. 223 : Administrative Report of the Ganjam Agency, 1884-85. Govt. Order, Judicial, 6 Aug. 1888, No. 1666. MacCartie's Report, *op. cit.*
14. GC File No. D. Dis. 26/1923 : Govt. Order, 27 May 1890, Miscellaneous Revenue, No. 3217. GC. File No. 20R/1905 : Report on Parlakhemundi *Maliahs* by A. W. Lushington, 18 Dec. 1905. Govt. Order No. 603, Development, 1 May 1922 : J. M. Turing to Govt., 25 Nov. 1920 and India

Despatch to Secretary of State, No. 38, 4 Aug. 1921 (Tamil Nadu Archives).

15. Proceedings of the Chief Conservator of Forests (Govt. of Madras), No. 555, Press, 9 December 1932 : Inspection Note on the Parlakhemundi Forests in Ganjam by F. R., Madan.
16. MJP, Govt. Order, No. 1099, 11 July 1899 : Administrative Report of the Ganjam Agency for 1898-99. In 1932, the Savaras of the Parlakhemundi Agency tract, who numbered 49,545 out of a total local population of 69,681, had not more than five per cent of the "permanently cultivated fields" for themselves. Madan's Report, *op. cit.*

16a GC. File No. 22D/1910. In 1932, M. Sheshadri, Asst. Collector, Ganjam, enquired into lands of the Kandhs held under mortgage by the non-hill men. He wrote "It is not so much the amount he initially borrows which is burdensome to the Kondh as the accumulation of interest brought about in the most devious way by the unscrupulous sowcar (money lender) GC. File No. 2830/1933 : Sheshadri's Report. MacCartie, Mounsey and Taylor reported the same too.

17. *Ibid.*
18. Thomson revised the *mamuls* in Parlakhemundi tribal tract in 1881-82; Mounsey did so in other parts of the Ganjam Agency at the same time. MacCartie completed Thomson's work. Taylor made further revisions in 1902. GC. File No. 3555/1925, Vol. I, Office Note, 10 Nov. 1930. Reports of MacCartie, Mounsey and Taylor, *op. cit.*
19. MacCartie's Report. "Government, I have always understood, insist very strongly upon the maintenance of the hereditary patro's authority in these hill tracts as an influential patro can render most valuable assistance and information in times of revolt which are always liable to occur. MacCartie to Agent, Ganjam, 30 June 1878.
20. This was particularly evident among the Kandhs of Ramgiri-Udaygiri and Chokpad. GC. File No. D. Dis. 2967/1921 S-3.
21. Boal, 1982, pp. 78-84, 181-9.
22. G. C. File No. R. Dis. 4197/1931, 1903/1934, 3555/1925, Vol. I.
23. GC. File No. 478/1917 : Board of Revenue Proceedings, No. 116, Misc. 24 Jan. 1917.
24. Madan's Report, *op. cit.*
25. GC. File No. 3555/1925, Vol. I. Mounsey's *Report, op. cit.*
26. GC. File No. D. Dis. 7597/1931 : Ganjam Agency Administration Report, 1931-32. *Ibid.* File No. 3985/1932.
27. GC. File No. R. Dis. 8698/1933. File No. 3611/1932. File No. 2705/1931. Ganjam Agency Administration Report, 1931/32, *op. cit.*

28. GC. File No. 1835/1934. In 1885, a very difficult five-mile *ghat* road from Possaro to Tentiligada was constructed by the Kandhs at Rs. 1,000, while in the plains such a work would have cost the Government at least Rs. 5,000. Ganjam Administration Report, 1884-85.

29. GC. File No. 6756/1926.

30. *Ibid.* GC. File No. D. Dis. 7593/1931. R. Dis. 1835/1934.

31. GC. File No. 2627/1933 : Agent's order.

32. Ganjam Agency Administration Report, 1931-32.

33. *Ibid.*, 1930-31, 1932-33. GC. File No. D. Dis. 1835/1934.

    M. Sheshari reported : "Whatever the safeguards provided by law, so long as the Kandh does not come to avail himself of these, the sowcar feels that he is safe in flouting the law ... he is confident of his hold over the Kandh ..... Of what consequence is the legality, if the Kandh does not take the matter up? G. C. File No. R. Dis. 2830/1933.

34. GC. File No. 6756, *op. cit.*

35. GC. File No. D. Dis. 10106/1931 : Govt. Order. Misc Revenue 205, 15 Dec. 1931. The length of the Government-maintained roads in the Agency in 1934 was 1,100 miles. GC. File No. 1835/1934.

36. GC. File No. R. Dis. 4197/1931.

37. The Government realised land revenue from only the lands acquired by the Oriya immigrants in the G. Udaygiru and Chokapad Agency tracts.

38. GC. File No. 2830/1933

39. GC. File No. 1835/1934 : Agency Office Note.

40. *Ibid.*

41. Ganjam Agency Administration Report, 1931-2.

42. Ganjam Agency Administration Report , 1932-3.

43. GC. File No. 1835/1934.

44. *Ibid.*

45. *Ibid.*

46. GC. File No. R. Dis. 7165/1932 : Govt. Order. Revenue Misc. 2696, 10 Sept. 1932. File No. 1835/1934 : Agency Office Note, 2 June 1934.

47. Govt. Order, Judicial, 1456, 19 Sept. 1868.

48. GC. File No. R. Dis. 2627/1933 : Agent's order. File No. R. Dis. 7165/1932: :Govt. Order Revenue Misc. 2696, 10 Sept. 1932.

49. GC. File No. R. Dis. 2627/1933, Agent's order.

50. GC. File No. 1835/1934. File No. R. Dis. 2627/1933, Agent's order. Ganjam Agency Administration Report, 1932-3.

51. G. C. File No. 3611/1934. File No. R. Dis. 2830/1933.
52. In Govt. Order No. 769, Revenue, 6 Apr. 1932, Panas were notified as a hill tribe for the operation of the Agency Tracts (Interest and Land Transfer) Act, 1917.
53. G. C. File No R. Dis. 2627/1933, Agency Office Note.

7

The Kutiya Kandh Uprising, 1865-1866

Tribal life does get transformed under the impact of an alien administration; that no doubt is inevitable. New forces released by the alien administration, also affect the time-honoured and cherished values of the tribals, setting off a strong reaction in them; that, too, is but natural. But then, both the nature and intensity of the reaction depend largely on the extent of the change desired by the administrator and the pace and agency of the change. The persistent problem in tribal administration is one of reconciliation of the interests of the government with the expectations of a people who for centuries had been the least governed and who want to be left alone. This problem was clearly reflected in the extensive Kandh uprising in the Chinnakimedi hill tracts in the Ganjam district in 1865-66.

Two groups of aboriginal people were involved in the uprising : the Kutiyas and the Parajas. The former, the wildest of all the Kandhs, lived in an area of two hundred square miles in Subarnagiri, the south-western part of the Chinnakimedi *maliah* (hill tract) under the Ganjam Agency administration. The Parajas, also a Kandh tribe, occupied an area of some eighty to one hundred and ten miles in the same *maliah* and an adjacent tract to the north called Mahasingi. The Parajas of Kalahandi, a neighbouring princely state in the Central Provinces, also joined the fray.

In their language, habits and dress, the Kutiyas considerably differed from the Parajas, looking down upon them as an inferior people. As for the Government, it viewed the Kutiyas as "the most uncertain of the hill tribes" [1] In 1857, they had risen in revolt against the Government's ban on human sacrifice, a cherished socio-religious practice having in the tribal mind an ample economic justification: the productivity of the soil had a direct and proportional relation to the sprinkling of human blood and the sowing of human flesh in it.

Fortunately, the disturbance then had been short-lived, thanks to the Government's own conciliatory policy and the intercession of some influential local tribal chiefs. The Government, with its hands full with the "Mutiny", chose neither to severely punish the Kutiya rebels nor disarm them; and this leniency it regretted in later years.[2]

Chinnakimedi *maliah* was the largest Kandh tract in the Ganjam Agency, being 1,975 square miles in extent,[3] as also the wildest; local tribesmen had the least contact with the British administration; the general policy of the Government was to let the wild men live their own life.

As elsewhere in the sprawling hill tracts of the Ganjam district, the Government ruled the Kutiya Kandh tracts through the agency of an Oriya elite. There was the zamindar and his subordinates, *patros*, *dalbeheras* and the *paiks*. The zamindar lived mostly in the plains, only occasionally going up the hills when the tribals gave him gifts as a token of their allegiance. Traditionally, the Oriya hill zamindar's authority in the Kutiya tract had been held more by his social influence than by overt military power, the tribals being as amenable to the one as resistant to the other. Over the years a number of Oriyas of the plains had entered the Kutiya hill tracts as itinerant traders in salt and as followers of the Oriya zamindar who used them as his militia.[4] These Oriya immigrants settled in tribal tracts where, with the encouragement of the zamindar, they became the keepers of law and order. The richer and more powerful of these Oriya immigrants consolidated their position under the local zamindar; with the official title *patro* and *bissoyi*, they held authority over the tracts allotted to them.

Having lived with the tribals for years, the Oriya elite naturally became an integral element of the local life, and this the British government made use of. The Government used the Oriya elite as doers of all work : maintenance of law and order, construction of roads, spreading education and suppressing barbarous socio-religious practices.

Roads being considered a military necessity, an economic artery and a civilising agency, their construction by cheap tribal labour was the responsibility of the Oriya elite. The *patros* sometimes paid the tribals engaged in roadworks either a small portion of the money they received from the Government for the works and sometimes no money at all, insisting on their customary right of getting free service from the tribals.[5]

The "civilising mission" of the British tribal administration drove a sharper wedge between the Oriya elite and the tribals. The latter intensely disliked the zeal of the *patros* and *paiks* in executing the Government's policy of suppressing human sacrifice and female infanticide, for this contrasted with the Oriya elite's traditional deference to these tribal institutions and their participation in tribal socio-religious observances. The elite, with the Government making use of them, emerged as the symbol of a new power to be grudgingly obeyed, greatly feared and intensely distrusted by the tribals whose natural tendency to resist the new grasping authority was balanced by their fear of the Government's military power in defence of the Oriya elite.

Indra Mohan Patro of Subarnagiri was the most influential Oriya chief of the Chinnakimedi *maliah* who had several sub-*patros* under him, each having his own sphere of authority over a cluster of tribal villages. The *patro* of Mahasingi, a minor, also had a number of subordinate *patros* to manage the local tribesmen.

In June 1865 the Subarnagiri *patro* was given a Government contract to construct a 15-mile road in his tract. The unsatisfactory progress of the work led the *patro* to send two Oriya village watchmen to persuade the local Kutiyas to expedite the work. The Kutiyas killed the two men and ignored the repeated admonition of the *patro*. The latter, as a conciliatory gesture, sent some grains to the Kutiyas through his Oriya subordinate staff, who, so the investigation later brought out, merrily appropriated most of them.[6] An insurrection developed fast, its avowed aim being the destruction and expulsion of all the local Oriyas. Several Oriya villages were set afire, their inhabitants killed and property looted. An Oriya child was sacrificed by the Kutiyas as a token of defiance of the Government's ban on human sacrifice.

Oriya retaliation that soon followed led to the destruction of many Kandh villages. Tumeribund, the *patro's* and the Agency Sub-Magistrate's headquarters, was the scene of many pitched battles before the *patro's* *paiks* and the local police could save it from the enraged tribals. Soon the Parajas of Mahasingi joined the Kutiyas, and then the Parajas of Kalahandi, all the tribals reportedly bound by *mutti*, "a kind of hereditary alliance, defensive and offensive" To make the matter worse, some British officers, caught napping, withdrew from their posts. By the time the Government woke up and its troops appeared on the scene, the southern and wilder parts of the Kutiya country had been cleared of the

Oriyas; but in the more populous and more accessible northern tracts, the Oriyas could manage to hold their own.

Before long, however, the situation was retrieved. The local police, aided by regular troops, combed the tribal tracts, decimating the rebels. Several Kandh leaders were rounded up; the Central Provinces authorities took care of the Kandh rebels in Kalahandi; finally, in February 1866 the Kutiya defiance ended.[7]

The police enquiry following the uprising brought out several facts; that the Government had no premonition of the trouble; that it had no adequate understanding of the tribal mind which was upset due to the socio-economic forces released by the British administration; that official machinery in the tribal tracts lacked coordination to function effectively; and that local officers' excessive zeal to transform the tribal life was at variance with the generally cautious policy of the Government itself at the highest level.

The disturbance caught the Government completely by surprise; it had not anticipated any difficulty in its road construction project—a project that had so long been an unqualified success, the Kandhs having worked with their natural alacrity and exertion. By July 1865 more than two hundred miles of road had been completed. Naturally, W. Robinson, the Inspector General of Police, Madras, hopefully reported his conviction that roads would not only enable the Government to explore the economic potentialities of the hill tracts, but in the process soon transform a "semi-barbarous and excitable population to the condition of peaceable and ordinary ryots". The men, Robinson had assured the Government, were "intelligent, industrious and hardworking, quite capable of being a civilised and producing people". All that was needed to accelerate the process was an annual investment of five thousand rupees for the road construction project.[8]

What Robinson failed to see was that, as in the Ghumsur hill tracts, the Government's road construction project had been successful wherever it could ensure immediate economic benefit to Kandh labourers; wherever it had failed to do so, Agency officers having given the local *patros* a free hand, the tribesmen had been cheated of their due wages.

In fact, in the Kutiya hill tract even British officers in charge of the road works had rather been overzealous in minimising both the cost of the project and the time of its execution; the construction of about two hundred and fifty mile road in a very difficult terrain had cost the

Government only fifteen rupees per mile, although the sanctioned cost was fifty rupees per mile.[9] Ganjam Agency officers had, in fact, acquiesced in what was patently the *patro* and *paik* oppression of the tribal labourers. This was clear from the report of R. C. A. Marshall, the Junior Assistant Agent in charge of the Chinnakimedi *maliahs* :

> That the roads are invaluable cannot be doubted, but to suppose that over 250 miles of road can be made and bridged in the short space of three or four months without oppression would be a great error.[10]

The Kandh labourers, Marshall pointed out, had been dragged twelve to fourteen miles away from their homes and compelled to work for more than a week at a stretch, and that in the agricultural season. This had angered the tribals far more than the pittance they received as wages, for they did not know the value of money.[11] Clearly, when the roads were being built very cheaply, the Government had chosen to overlook the causal relationship between the Oriya elite's zeal to extend the communication system in tribal tracts, the reinforcement of their economic hold on the tribals and the simmering tribal discontent. The oppression of the police constables supervising the construction work made the matters worse;[12] and this important fact did not figure in the Inspector General's report to the Government.

Obviously, the *patros* and the *paiks,* as agents of the Government, had been assuming far more authority and power than sanctioned by tribal tradition. As collaborators of the powerful British government, the Oriya elite had little fear of tribal resistance to their oppression, sure as they were of protection by the Government. The Kutiya uprising was the tribal reaction to the new role assumed by the Oriya elite as the agents of the Government; hence the Kandhs' "insubordinate feelings towards the Oriya patros" and their "ill-will towards immigrant races in general" whose exploitation of the tribals had coincided with the consolidation of the British administration in Ganjam hill tracts.[13]

Robinson's enquiry further revealed that the "civilising mission" of the Government was yet to achieve its declared object : socio-religious reclamation of the aboriginals. For example, despite the exertion of Meriah Agency for fifteen years,[14] the Kandhs retained their faith in the efficacy of human sacrifice as a deterrent to droughts and epidemics. "It may well be feared that the hearty, but now checked, longing for human blood is sacrcely less strong than it was", so reported the Inspector-General. Even a number of influential *patros* admitted to

Robinson that but for the fear of punishment by the Government, the rite, suspended for a time, "would revive very generally throughout the hills".[15]

In fact, the Kutiya Kandh uprising coincided with an unprecedented agricultural distress in Ganjam and the rest of Orissa, culminating in a worst ever famine. This only deepened the Kandh conviction "no *meriah,* no rain," and so their pent-up wrath fell upon the Oriya *patros* and *paiks,* who were instrumental in suppressing this "national religion", and who, as agents of the Government, were the main obstacles to its revival.[16]

The *panas*, originally immigrants from the foothills, who were the traditional procurers of *meriahs* and whose livelihood had been affected by the Government's ban on the rite, fanned the Kandh resentment against the Oriya elite. But then, the enraged Kandhs hated the *panas* no less than the Oriyas, for they too, as petty traders, moneylenders and at places even landgrabbers, had been exploiting the Kandhs. No wonder the Kandh wrath fell also on the *panas* who made a common cause with the Oriyas for mutual defence.

The Kandhs knew that the Government had kept many rescued *meriahs*[17] and their children in the custody of local *patros*. They also knew of many famished Oriyas in the foothills and plains eager to sell their children as *meriahs* if only the rite could be resumed and rains brought in thereby.[18]

The Kandhs had genuine economic grievances. Cheap rice in the thinly populated hills had over the years encouraged Oriya and *pana* immigration from the foothills and plains; the new men carried on a lucrative trade in rice plunging the local Kandhs in acute distress, especially in the lean years. Thus, in 1866 not more than seventeen seers of rice could be had for a rupee in the Kutiya Kandh tracts when normally seventy seers of rice, was the rate. The Agency administration, in its turn, insisted on the supply of cheap rice by the local *patros* without much bothering about the latter's extorting its tribal growers.[19]

Official lapses aggravated the Kutiya discontent, if not caused it. Captain Marshall, the Junior Assistant Agent, Chinnakimedy *maliahs*, scarcely visited the wild Kutiya tracts, confining his official tours to Kandh settlements in the foothills and the plains. Robinson even charged Marshall with dereliction of duty; he did not even go to the scene of disturbance as often as was needed, and he was inactive at Tumeribund, an important post.[20] Inspector Glasson fled in panic from Gumagarh, another important post; all this had been a shot in the arm for the rebels.[21]

Worst of all, despite the inadequacy of the general police arrangement in the Ganjam district, the Madras government had made a ten per cent cut in the local police establishment in 1863-64.[22] Besides there was no effective check on police constables working hand in glove with oppressive *patros* and *paiks*. The Kutiya tract itself had in it no police or any other public establishment at the time of the uprising, while the local *patro's* authority had been considerably affected by the incessantly squabbling sub-*patros*,[23] the men responsible for the maintenance of law and order.

The uprising led to no great change in the Madras Government's tribal policy except that it would observe greater caution in executing the policy. The Government would now establish closer and more direct contact with the tribesmen through British officers and their staff, such a measure having worked well in the Ghumsur hill tracts, Digi, Baramutha and Daringabadi where the local Kandhs seemed to have been reconciled to the local administration.[24] The Oriya elite would continue to enjoy the Government's patronage but brought under closer Government supervision to prevent too palpable abuse of power. The Government's main concern hereafter was to adjust the relations between the Oriya elite and the tribesmen with a view to increasing the former's efficiency as the main catalytic force used by the local administration and the latter's willing acquiescence in the inevitable growth of the local Oriya elite's authority. The Government would keep opening up the tribal tracts by roads to promote trade and commerce and facilitate Oriya immigration from the plains as the most potent means of "civilising" the tribals.

Hereafter, the Assistant Agent, the Assistant Superintendent of Police and their staff would reside in the Chinnakimedi hills for a period of six to eight months in a year with their headquarters at Baliguda. The police establishment was strengthened with one hundred more men, and an additional Inspector was provided to the Ganjam police establishment; the police men would now be given a special allowance for hill duty.[25] Some *panas* employed by the Government as village watchmen, who had abused their power, were dismissed from service while loyal *patros* who had helped the Government to restore peace were rewarded. The *patros* were henceforth required to supply lesser quantity of supplies for the Agency staff at a better price,[26] the Government hoping that they would not extort the Kandh farmers as hitherto. The Government also decided to detach the Chinnakimedi *maliahs* from the control of the Chinnakimedi zamindar, thereby asserting a new principle in tribal administration : the Oriya elite's failure to maintain law and order in their tribal tracts would result in the Government's direct control of the tracts. However, not until 1872 were the *maliahs* formally resumed by the Government.[27]

The Madras civil servants regarded the measures taken as enough, but not the Governor, Lord Napier, who assumed power shortly after the Kutiya rebellion had been quelled. Napier was critical of his subordinates' very approach to the issue and particularly of Robinson's enquiry report. He condemned the report as lacking in the "stamp of completeness, reflection and impartiality, "the Inspector-General being particularly careful in making light of the responsibility of the police in the disturbance. It did not escape Napier's attention that while in Marshall's report the oppression of the Kandhs by the local Oriya elite and the police figured prominently as the cause of the disturbance, Robinson attributed it solely to the unruly temper of the tribals and their natural antipathy to the "immigrant races" in general.

Napier wanted a special commission of enquiry to not only make an on-the-spot investigation of the causes of the outbreak, but suggest measures to prevent its recurrence in future. Suppression of the disturbance was not enough; to him the Government's main task was to win the confidence and attachment of the tribals. This clearly had not been achieved. Napier's tours in the Ganjam district convinced him that the Kutiyas had been "only half-subdued and that they remained more deeply alienated from British authority than at any previous period".

Napier viewed the uprising as a reflection on the very nature of the tribal administration as it then existed and more particularly on the Government's use of the Oriya elite as its main agency of change in tribal life. He saw nothing unnatural in the tribal reaction against "the encroachment of a superior race", the Oriyas, and "the innovations of a civilised government", "the aggressive influences" of both being correlated and coeval. Not that Napier would give up the existing policy of changing the tribal life nor would he dispense with the services of the Oriya elite for the purpose, but he would take a close and critical look at the implementation of the policy in order to prevent any gross abuse of power by the Oriya elite.[28]

The Madras civil servants, however, were opposed to any on-the-spot enquiry by a special commission, particularly so soon after the uprising had been quelled. Any such step was likely to unsettle the tribal mind and militate against the measures taken to pacify them. Napier was not quite impressed by this line of argument, but he chose to acquiesce when, Thomas Pycroft, his colleague in the Council, supported the contention of the Madras officers.[29]

What followed was but natural; roads continued to tear into hitherto inaccessible tracts, Oriya *patros* as contractors for road works making hay when the Sun shone. Trade and commerce developed slowly no doubt, but along with came more immigrants from the plains to settle in tribal tracts. For the present, the Government viewed it as a welcome development; civilised men of the plains would make the tribals better human beings. But a time lay not far off when the Government would itself realise that unchecked Oriya immigration into tribal tracts created problems. It indeed affected the Government's long term interests in tribal tracts as it harmed tribal interests. The Government then faced a new problem : how to help retain tribal identity in the face of the overwhelming impact of the activities of the agents of The Government—the Oriya elite.

Notes and References

1. MJP, 20 Mar. 1866, No. 142 : W. Robinson, Inspector-General of Police, Madras, to Chief Secretary, Madras, 24 Jan. 1866. *Madras Manual of Administration,* Vol. I (Madras, 1885), p. 73
2. Robinson to Chief Secretary, Madras, *op. cit.*
3. Maltby, *op. cit.,* p. 20.
4. H. Mounsey, *History of the Ganjam Maliahs : Information regarding the Special Agent's Disivion* (Madras, 1884), p. 2. The ancestors of the Oriya Chiefs belonged to Baud. Madras Manual, *op. cit.,* p. 74.
5. See pp. 63-64,66 above.
6. Robinson to Chief Secretary, *op. cit.*
7. *Ibid.*
8. MJP, 23 Dec. 1865, Nos. 194-5 : Robinson to Chief Secretary, 17 July, 9 Aug. 1865.
9. In March 1865, following outbreaks in the Kandh and Savara tracts in 1863-4, the Government had sanctioned the construction of a 370-mile road in the Ganjam tribal tracts at a cost of fifty rupees a mile. MJP, 21 Mar. 1865, Nos. 152-3.
10. MJP, 8 May 1866, No. 108 : Marshall to Agent, Ganjam, 10 Mar. 1866.
11. *Ibid.*

12. *Ibid.*
13. Robinson to Chief Secretary, 24 Jan. 1866, *op. cit.*
14. See pp. 22-23 above.
15. Robinson to Chief Secretary, 24 Jan. 1866, *op. cit.*
16. *Ibid.*
17. Till 1861, when the Meriah Agency was wound up, the Government had rescued some 1,400 *meriahs* from Ghūmsur and Chinnakimedi tribal tracts. *Madras Manual, op. cit.*, p. 72f.n.
18. Robinson to Chief Secretary, 24 Jan. 1866, *op. cit.*
19. MJP, 20 Mar. 1866, No. 145 : Robinson to Chief Secretary, 21 Jan. 1866.
20. MJP, 8 May 1866, No. 107 : Inspector-General, Madras Police (Robinson) to Agent, Ganjam, 30 Jan. 1866, and Agent, Ganjam to Chief Secretary, 8 Feb. 1866. Marshall was later censured and replaced.
21. Robinson to Chief Secretary, 21 Jan. 1866, *op. cit.*
22. Robinson to Chief Secretary, 28 Feb. 1866; *op. cit.*
23. Robinson to Chief Secretary, 24 Jan. 1866.
24. *Ibid.*
25. MJP, 20 Mar. 1866, No. 46 : Govt. Order, No. 403, 20 Mar. 1866.
26. Robinson to Chief Secretary, 28 Feb. 1866, *op. cit.*
27. MJP, 20 Mar. 1866 : Govt. Order, 20 Mar. 1866, No. 403, Mounsey, *op. cit.* p. 5.
28. *Minutes Recorded by Baron Napier During his Administration of the Madras Presidency from 1866 to 1872* (Madras, 1873), pp. 60-65.
29. *Ibid.*

8

Bamra, Patna and Kalahandi, 1868-1882: Tribal Peasant Discontent in Western Orissa

Discontent among the tribal peasantry in Bamra, Patna and Kalahandi, all feudatory states in western Orissa and under the authority of the government of the Central Provinces, varied in intensity but bore some common features. The commonness lay as much in the origin of the discontent and its aggravation as in its course and character. The British government's measures to tackle the crises and the consequences of tribal discontent in the three states had also some commonness in them. In the last four decades of the 19th century tribal peasant discontent posed a problem for the local British authorities in the districts of Ganjam, Vizagapatam and East Godavari, all under the Madras government. One would see a pattern in the peasant discontent in the tribal tracts of western Orissa and those in parts of the Madras Presidency now called Andhra Pradesh.[1]

The origin of the tribal discontent in Bamra, Patna and Kalahandi could be traced to several factors—geographical features of the three states, their ethnic composition, historical tradition and administrative set up. Hills and forests covered a large part of the states, rendering their close administration both difficult and expensive. Considering their territorial extent, the revenue realised from the states was small. The local tribal population—Kandhs mainly—was still unintegrated with the growing Oriya population of the states, mostly immigrants from the plains.

The Kandh tradition had it that they were the original inhabitants of the three states which through the centuries had been colonised gradually by Hindu princely families, especially in the wake of the Muslim conquest of northern and central India in the 14th and 15th centuries. These families emerged in course of time as the rulers of the tribal states. However, in the beginning, the new Hindu rulers were neither able nor disposed to impose any direct authoritv on the local people whose management was left as before to tribal headmen, whose main job was to maintain law and order and settle disputes.

In course of time, Oriyas from the foothills and plains came to the states and settled there as farmers, traders and money lenders, the rulers encouraging the settlement. The growth of non-tribal, mostly Oriya, population in the states was accompanied by large scale alienation of tribal lands to the Oriyas whom the rulers made zamindars of extensive tracts, officers of the states and even village headmen, called *gaontias*, charged with the responsibility of collecting revenues. The traditional power, position and authority of Kandh leaders tended to decline in proportion to the prosperity of the Oriya immigrants. Oriya zamindars and their followers levied many cesses on the tribals which had no sanction in local tradition. Seething discontent was the natural tribal reaction to Oriya oppression.

This development antedated the establishment of British authority in western Orissa in 1818 when the Maratha rule there ended,[2] but the trend of Oriya oppression of the local tribals aggravated during the British rule. The rulers of western Orissa had their internal and external security guaranteed by the paramount British Government, which generally desisted from interference in the internal administration of the feudatory states. This gave some rulers a virtually free hand to mistreat their subjects, of whom the tribals formed a large segment. Only in the event of tribal discontent escalating into a large scale disturbance would the British government intervene. Even such intervention had but a limited object : to remove the immediate causes of the tribal discontent, to adjust the conflicting interests of the parties involved in the crisis and to remedy the glaring defects in the local administration affecting the tribal life. No long term measure to prevent tribal discontent in future was adopted by the British government.

In all the three states tribal discontent kept pace with power struggles in the ruling families of the states. All the scrambling families made the fullest use of their tribal followers to gain their object. This tribal involvement was a factor not only in the familial quarrels but in the disaffection to the British government borne by some disgruntled elements in the families. In such circumstances, while dealing with the tribal discontent in a feudatory state, the British government had also to compose the internecine quarrels in the ruling family of the state as also to redress its grievances against the Government.

Invariably, the Government's policy was to put some restraint on the erstwhile unbridled powers of the rulers to oppress their tribal subjects. The Government would also take over the administration of some states for a time to implement some new measures, the object being to adjust the tribal-non-tribal relations in the state. Tribal interests would generally be safeguarded without greatly impairing the power and influence of the local non-tribals, mostly Oriyas.

Though varying in extent, population and resources, the three states, Bamra, Patna and Kalahandi, had a common problem : simmering discontent in the local Kandh peasantry under an unfeeling, oppressive administration.

Bamra lay about twenty miles from Sambalpur, being under the jurisdiction of the Deputy Commissioner of Sambalpur. About four hundred square miles in area, only one-sixth of the state was under cultivation; hilly tracts covered a large part of the state. Scattered in about two hundred hamlets on the hills lived the Kandhs, numbering about 1200, who had much in common with the Kandhs of Ghumsur, Baud, Angul and Kalahandi.[2a] Human sacrifice used to be a common practice among them till the British government banned it. The Bamra ruler's relations with his Kandh subjects was rather tenuous; "more formal than real";[3] the subordination of these subjects to the ruler had just one form : the latter receiving on ceremonial occasions some gifts from his subjects.[3a] The ruler relied on a local zamindar, an Oriya, to manage the Kandhs. The zamindar and his family wielded great influence on the Kandhs who were his followers. There was no love lost between the Bamra ruler and the zamindar, the latter, with the support of his tribal followers, often defying the authority of the ruler.

What particularly drew the attention of the British government to the small feudatory state was the involvement of the zamindar family in the revolt of 1857, the leader of which in the Sambalpur region was Surendra Sai.[4] Srikrishna Behera the zamindar, and his Kandh followers had stood solidly behind Surendra Sai; he preferred being burnt alive to surrendering to the Government the rebels he had sheltered. As a punitive measure the British government took over the Kandh tracts, forcing the two younger brothers of the zamindar, Krupasindhu and Dharanee to flee; the two men then assumed the leadership of the local Kandhs. About this time, the British seized the eldest son of Srikrishna and hanged him at Sambalpur on a charge of murdering his wife. This further embittered Krupasindhu and Dharanee, who incited their Kandh followers to create troubles for the Bamra ruler, an ally of the British Government.[5]

The Government had no intention to be militarily involved in the quarrels between the Bamra ruler and the zamindar's family. It rather preferred to assuage the family's wrath and compose its feud with the ruler, it being the best means to restore peace in the state. Accordingly, an amnesty was declared, the Government declaring Krupasindhu as the zamindar of the Kandh tract while, his brother Dharanee, was made the *Dewan* of the Bamra state. This arrangement remained undisturbed till 1863 when trouble recrudesced.[6]

The trouble originated in the attachment of some villages in Krupasindhu's zamindary by the Bamra ruler after the Sambalpur Court directed him to do so. The Court upheld the contention of a local merchant from whom Krupasindhu's late brother, Srikrishna, had taken a loan and had mortgaged three villages to the creditor who held them in possession till 1857. During the disturbances that year, the merchant had fled somewhere; he returned some years later and sought to occupy the villages. By this time, however, the Government had pardoned Krupasindhu and given him possession of his estate including the three villages mortgaged to the merchant. Now Krupasindhu would neither pay up the loan incurred by his late brother nor restore the three villages to the merchant who thereupon filed a suit in the Sambalpur Court. In 1866, when the Bamra ruler made over the villages under the Court's order, Krupasindhu fled to the hills and incited the Kandhs against the ruler. With his tribal followers he plundered villages, spreading panic and ultimately obliging the ruler to ask police support from the British government. The police could at first achieve a limited success; it restored order but only for a while. Krupasindhus, unabated depredations and the Bamra ruler's unceasing requests for more police assistance created a problem for the Government.[7]

The Government's reaction was more one of embarrassment than worry. Such small crises in feudatory states it wanted the local rulers to tackle themselves instead of seeking support from the Government, The Government would prefer a political settlement of the trouble to any military involvement in a tract which was far from well known and against a people whose "distinguishing characteristic" was believed to be "passionate love of liberty and . . . devotion to their chiefs."[8]

But then, the Government could not ignore the fact that the trouble was certainly not of the ruler's own making. Local official reports described him as

> quiet and unassuming, but shrewd and intelligent withal. He managed his affairs very well and is . . . particularly kind to the people and appears to be much liked by them.[9]

His only fault was his "lack of firmness and determination" to deal with the traditionally refractory elements in the state. In fact, Major Cumberledge, the Deputy Commissioner, Sambalpur, tried to instil confidence in him but failed in his purpose. The ruler's heart had sunk lower still when several zamindars in the state saved villages from plunder by Krupasindhu and his Kandh followers by paying them sums of money. So panicked the ruler was that he was even prepared to make over the state to the British with the hope that they would deal with Krupasindhu firmly, restore order in the state and then give the state back to the ruler.[10]

In such circumstances the Government was obliged to send a small force with definite instructions to avoid as long as possible armed encounters with the Kandhs and to defuse the crisis by political means. Lt. Bowrie, commanding the force, made personal appeals to Krupasindhu to make up with the Bamra ruler. Alongside he sought to detach the Kandhs from Krupasindhu and to isolate and weaken him thereby. Bowrie freely mixed with the Kandhs, the first local British officer to do so, seeking to remove their deep-set fear of the Government. Bowrie urged the Kandhs to recognise Kamallochan, a minor grandson of Srikrishna, as the new zamindar and to desert Krupasindhu and his brother, now declared outlaws by the Government.[11]

The Chief Commissioner of the Central Provinces, George Campbell, however, was anxious to avoid any complications with the Kandhs if the Government foisted on them another zamindar. Campbell's policy was distinctly conciliatory :

> Action is to be confined to the defensive and nothing aggressive is to be undertaken in the Khond country .... great care be taken not to get too far into the hills or fall into any scrape.[12]

He wanted the local authorities to offer pardon to the trouble makers and induce them to surrender.

The Bamra ruler's failure to manage his Kandh tracts led the Chief Commissioner to decide to bring the tracts under the direct management of the Government.[12a] In almost identical circumstances the Government had taken over from the *raja* of Angul his Kandh tracts in 1849.

Bowrie's measures proved successful. Gradually many Kandh followers of Krupasindhu and his brother surrendered. Some members of the rebel zamindar's family were captured and kept under the custody of the Bamra ruler as a guarantee of Krupasindhu's good behaviour in future. Major Cumberledge was confident that the crisis had passed off; the rebel zamindars, band of followers had been broken up, rendering him incapable of any more mischief. Krupasindhu was now unlikely to get a safe refuge in the Kandh hills, for the local men had been largely won over by the Government.[13]

One result of the short expedition was the first hand knowledge, the Government acquired of the Kandh tracts and the local people. The tracts were indeed very wild and difficult; Cumberledge and his men had to literally cut their way through the region. The soil, however, was exceedingly rich; rice, cotton, castor oil and pulses were the main products; the method of cultivation was locally called *dhya*, slash and burn.[14]

The first hand knowledge of the Kandhs of Bamra established that the Government's earlier impression of the men was wrong : the men were, in fact, far different from the wild Kandhs, a violent and volatile people. The latter whom Cumberlege called the *usl* Kandhs or pure-bred Kandhs, were a "determined and courageous race" who would "stand by each other to the last." The Bamra Kandhs, by contrast, were really "a thievish and cowardly set", who deserted their Hindu leader, the rebel zamindar, when the Government police appeared on the scene.[15]

The Government abandoned the earlier scheme of taking over the Kandh tracts, for local reports discounted the possibility of any crises in future when the zamindar's influence had been ended and the Kandhs won over by the local officers.[16] It was now the Bamra ruler's responsibility to manage the tribal tracts more effectively. The Government would help the ruler by bridging the existing communication gap between him and his tribal subjects. The refractory zamindar had made use of this gap to misrepresent to the Kandhs the policies of the ruler and the British government and to sow in them a feeling of bitterness against both.

Cumberledge took the Bamra ruler along with him while scurrying through the Kandh tracts, in the process convincing the tribals that for the powerful British government no region was inaccessible. Since the Bamra ruler had never oppressed the Kandhs and since the latter had "nothing particularly truculent about them",[17] local authorities hoped that soon good relations would develop between the ruler and his tribal subjects. Hereafter the Government would encourage the ruler to take active interest in his tribal subjects while preventing any abuse of authority by him. The policy paid off; peace and order soon returned to the state.

Patna, a feudatory state in the Central Provinces, covered an area of 4,500 square miles; it had an annual revenue of less than 13,000 rupees, of which 600 rupees were paid to the British government as tribute. The Kandh tracts of the state, called Kondhan, was about 700 square miles in extent, of which three-fifths were cultivated. 20,000 people lived in the tract, three-fifths being Kandhs living in 400 villages. These Kandhs had not quite acquiesced in their subjection to the ruler of Patna and had in the past resisted any attempt at oppression by the latter. Government reports described the hill Kandhs of the Patna state as "wild and excitable, totally uncivilised and, when roused, prone to deeds of blood."[18] The Gohunka Kandhs of Belgaon were the most troublesome, a sulky and discontented lot of people.[19]

The Kandhs of the plains of the state had long-standing grievances against the ruler's oppression, the exactions of his *paiks* and revenue officers, and the increasing economic disabilities they suffered at the hands of immigrant non-tribals; gross violation of time-honoured tribal traditions angered the Kandhs most. And such violation was best represented in the change effected by the ruler in the local land revenue administration.

Traditionally, the ruler used to collect land revenue from each zamindary in the state through local tribal chiefs and village headmen. This practice was gradually abandoned with the decline in the authority of the tribal patriarchs. Thereafter, every zamindary was parcelled out into shares of four or five villages, each having the collateral descendants of the original patriarch's family. The authority of each share was vested in the actual holder of the tracts, irrespective of the local tribal head, who had only his share assigned to him, and whose claim to superior rank lay in the fact that he collected the revenue and remitted it to the ruler of the state.[20]

In course of time the ruler had recognised many immigrant Oriya farmers as zamindars and *gaontias* as revenue collectors who appropriated to themselves extensive tribal tracts and even some rent-free official tenures, called *bhogra*.

In Patna, Brahmins from Ganjam and Karans from Cuttack were the local money lenders, not the Marwaris, as elsewhere. Other castes, telis and bhuliyas, mainly, also had extensive money lending business as also many Oriya *gaontias*.[21] Over the years these *gaontias* had systematically ousted many defaulting tribal ryots from their ancestral lands. Since the gaontias were obliged to remit revenue collections to the ruler of the state, they settled many Oriya ryots in erstwhile Kandh tracts, they being a hardy and enterprising people, who paid their dues in time; by contrast, the local Kandh peasants, chary of hard work, were habitual defaulters.

The dispossessed Kandh ryots, who for a time moved to other areas, returned to their ancestral lands and pressed the *gaontias* to restore them. For, according to the Kandh tradition, the priority of occupation alone was the basis of the right to land, and no break in the occupation, whether voluntary or enforced, and however long that may have lasted, ever destroyed a man's right to the land which his ancestors had occupied when the Kandhs came to the state centuries ago. The Oriya *gaontias* and Oriya ryots refused to recognise this tradition, and instead advanced the new idea of the right to land belonging to those who made regular payment of the revenue demand.[22] Unlike before, these land disputes could no longer be amicably settled by tribal patriarchs, for their authority and influence had greatly waned. These disputes would now be settled in Government courts, involving the delay and expense which the Kandhs could hardly afford. The Kandh peasant's economic plight was further aggravated by cesses of many kinds which the ruler of the state and his hirelings imposed on him.

The Kandh peasants had "no command of money", and the absence of a ready market for the disposal of any surplus local products aggravated the stagnancy of their economy. Little wonder, the Kandhs lived in "abject poverty", being "without grains to eat, seed to sow or cattle to plough with." And all this when their land was "the fairest and most fertile."[23]

In 1868-69, when the ruler died, the state faced a crisis. Sur Pratap Deo, the new ruler, had already besotted and enfeebled himself by drug addiction, thus becoming unfit for administration. His brother exacted cesses from Kandh peasants, forcing them to flee to the neighbouring state of Kalahandi. Disgusted with oppression, the Kandhs made an abortive attempt on his life and killed his *paiks* sent to collect cesses.

The Kandhs also looted some Oriya traders and killed two Muslim merchants. Lala Biswanath Singh, the ruler's brother, struck in vengeful retaliation, assisted by the *paiks* sent by the ruler of Kalahandi, Udit Pratap Deo, who had family relation with the ruling house of Patna.[24]

The orgy of violence, particularly on Kandh women and children, drew the Government's intervention. Biswanath Singh was removed to Sambalpur and kept there under surveillance. The Patna ruler's "cruelty, apathy and timidity" had brought the administration to such a pass that its take over by the paramount power was the only course left. What angered the Government most was the reported performance of the rite of human sacrifice by the ruler to propitiate the family deity before dealing with the insurgent Kandh peasantry.[25] The ruler was guilty not only of inability to administer his state but defiance of the suzerain authority which had banned the rite throughout the tribal tracts of India.

Kalahandi, also called Karonde, came under the British suzerainty in 1854 following the annexation of the state of Nagpur, of which it was a dependency. In extent 3,745 square miles and with a population of 2,24,548, according to the 1881 census, the annual revenue of the state was 1,26,000 rupees of which 3,250 rupees were paid by the state as tribute to the British government.[26] Kalahandi was under the jurisdiction of the Chattisgarh Agency of the Central Provinces. Next to Bastar, it was the most important feudatory state in the province.

The state had two revenue divisions, the *Khalsa*, under the direct administration of the ruling chief, and the five zamindaries in feudal relationship with the chief to whom each of them paid a fixed annual tribute.[27]

The Kalahandi *khalsa* was bounded on the north by another feudatory state, Patna; the ruling families of the two states had matrimonial relation. To the east of Kalahandi lay the vast tribal tract of Chinnakimedi and the feudatory state of Baud, under the Madras and Bengal governments respectively. To the north was the extensive Jeypore zamindari in the Vizagapatnam district under the Madras government.

All these neighbouring tracts of Kalahandi were largely populated by Kandhs, though not all the tribesmen were at the same level of development. They, however, shared a common antipathy to overt and sudden assaults on their traditional institutions by an alien administration. The Kandhs' strong feeling of kinship surfaced during their conflicts with alien agents of change when discontent in a section of the tribe could escalate into a general tribal revolt encompassing a wide area. This is what happened in Kalahandi in 1881-82.

For many years the Kandhs were discontented due to the progressive loss of their land to immigrant Oriya farmers and the systematic destruction of their traditional institutions by the ruler of Kalahandi, Udit Pratap Deo, whose land revenue policy, in particular, proved detrimental to the accustomed tribal economy.

The Kandhs claimed the ownership of the entire tract of the Kalahandi state, which over the centuries they had cleared of dense forests. Tradition had it that sometime in the twelfth century the Kandhs had invaded the tract from the south and driven out the local tribe, the "Bathras". The Kandhs had then parcelled out the plain lands among themselves, each clan or group of families taking possession of a separate area which they called *desh*, naming it after the clan holding it. Each clan, occupying a *desh* or circle of villages had a headman, called *Umrao* to whom each village headman, called *majhi*, owed absolute allegiance. The *Umrao* exercised great influence on the Kandh peasant life, having the last word in all matters in his circle of villages.[28]

Originally the Kandh peasants paid no rent or tax of any kind other than small presents to the *Umraos* on specific occasions, such as after the settlement of disputes by them. The right to land was inalienable; for any crime whatever, eviction from holdings was impossible. Land for the Kandh peasant was not just the means of economic security but the strongest bond of kinship too; it was a part of his spiritual and economic heritage; it provided him with the very emotional basis of his being. Even the *Umraos* and *majhis* tilled their holdings themselves; there was no landlord in tribal agrarian economy.

Traditionally, the Kandhs of Kalahandi, like those of other neighbouring feudatory states in western Orissa, claimed that their ancestors had laid the foundation of the state by enabling a Hindu Rajput dynasty to set up its rule in the region—and that several centuries ago. Every ruler of Kalahandi had undergone a tribal investiture ceremony in which the hereditary Kandh chief, called *patmajhi*, had made the new ruler sit on his lap and tied a piece of cloth around his head, signifying the tribal acceptance of his rule. The Kandhs believed that this traditional ceremony was the public acknowledgement of the fact that every ruler of the state was appointed by the tribesmen themselves rather than succeeded to the throne by any right of inheritance.[29]

The ruling chiefs of Kalahandi and their underlings, the Oriya zamindars and *gaontias,* formed an important element in the Kandh political structure in which both the tribals and the Oriyas had a clearly defined and recognised position. The Kandh peasants acknowledged the suzerainty of the chiefs without having to suffer their rigorous political control. Until the middle of the 19th century, the Chief's authority in the Kandh tracts was remote and scarcely felt, and so it was willingly borne by the tribesmen, for whose sentiments, traditions and institutions, the Chief and the Oriya elite functioning under him showed both a deep understanding and due deference.

The only manifestation of the Chief's suzerainty lay in his Kandh subjects presenting him and his Oriya officers some gifts on fixed occasions, and the Chief presenting ceremonial clothes to *Umraos* and *majhis* when they assumed power as such.

The *Umrao* was the traditional medium of communication between the Chief and the tribal peasantry, he being responsible for the collection of land revenue and its payment to the Chief's treasury. For this service he received free service *(bhet beggar),* and offerings of rice and goat by tribal peasants in his *desh.*

The *Umraos* and *majhis* maintained the general law and order in tribal tracts; their loyalty to Kalahandi rulers was the surest guarantee of the position they held. The Kalahandi rulers and the local Oriya aristocracy often used their Kandh followers in their power struggles and in settling inter-familial scores. This aggravated inter-clan disputes in the tribal society.

As elsewhere, in Kalahandi too, there were Kandhs who lived in the plains and valleys of the state, and others who lived in the hills; the latter, called the Kutiyas, were a far fiercer people with little communication with the people of the plains and non-tribals in general.

The relations between the ruler of Kalahandi, Udit Pratap Deo,[30] and his Oriya subordinates on the one hand and the local Kandh peasantry on the other progressively changed following the state's reduction as a feudatory of British India. The new suzerain authority not only demanded from the ruler an enhanced annual tribute, but its regular and punctual payment as well. The Chief's life style too changed in course of time following his attachment to the British government; he needed new luxuries with which to entertain visiting British officers; he undertook extensive trips; he sent his relatives to schools for education. All this called for new means of raising revenue. He brought Oriya farmers and settled them in the state as a means of extending cultivation and increasing the land revenue yield.

Udit Pratap was highly rated by the British government which viewed stability in the administration as a measure of its efficiency, the mark of stability being the absence of widespread uprising. The British government gave the Chief a free hand, without regard to whether it fell heavily on his subjects; the latter's inability to openly express their discontent was mistaken by the British government as their willing acquiescence in the rule. Udit Pratap provided the Government with just what it wanted in a feudatory state—a strong personalised administration which ensured the regular and timely payment of tribute. The increasing revenue of the state was the sign of its growing prosperity; the British government seemed to have had no concern over the systematic spoliation of the Kandh peasantry and their muffled discontent.

Udit Pratap ruled with an iron hand, being particularly exacting in dealing with his Kandh subjects. He encouraged the immigrant Oriya farmers, called *kultas*, to oust Kandh *Umraos* and *majhis* from their tracts. The Oriyas took possession of the best available lands, reducing their original Kandh owners to mere ploughmen whose indebtedness to *kulta* money lenders made their plight worse. The *kultas* were expert farmers but hard landlords, good at extending agriculture but merciless in rackrenting and dispossessing the impoverished Kandh peasants.[31]

Udit Pratap imposed on his subjects a heavy land tax which the thrifty, enterprising, and resourceful Oriya farmers could alone pay—and this justified his preference for these men. He recognised some *kultas* as *gaontias* and village headmen, replacing the Kandh *majhis*; the *kultas* were also given *bhogra* or rent-free land.

Udit Pratap's policy was to systematically break the *Umraos'* traditional position in the Kandh society and to bring the tribals under closer control of the Oriya landed aristocracy favoured by him. He changed the traditional land revenue administration, in the process increasing his revenue demand and impairing the *Umrao's* accustomed position. Earlier, the *desh* or circle of villages was the unit of administration. The *Umraos* used to be assessed in lump sum for their respective *desh*; they themselves apportioned the assessment among villages under their authority; and they nominated the *majhis*. Now, Udit Pratap fixed the land revenue on each village; the *Umrao* was just the collector of revenue.[32]

Udit Pratap also discontinued the long-established practice of distributing to the *Umraos* on ceremonial occasions pieces of cloth, thus denying the men what they had so long cherished as a symbol of special treatment by the Chief of the state who recognised the special position of the *Umraos* in Kandh society. The Oriya officers of the Chief and the *kultas* would now deal directly with the Kandh peasants and not through the local *Umraos* as before.[33]

Udit Pratap maintained a band of Oriya armed retainers, called *paiks* whose services were frequently sought by the state police to oversee the law and order situation in tribal villages. For their services the *paiks* were given rent-free land on a fixed scale; besides an amount of grain from villages under their supervision. Over the years the *paiks* had acquired more lands than originally given to them as service tenure, and invariably these lands originally belonged to Kandh peasants. To cap all, the Kalahandi chief had imposed a variety of cesses on tribal peasants which were without the sanctity of any tradition whatever.[34]

The grasping nature of Udit Pratap's rule was evident, in particular, in the last six years of his rule when there "was no one too high or too low to feel his hand";

> he raised the assessment of the villages in the khalsa to the highest pitch it could be strained; he put a tax on everything which was susceptible to taxation, and he systematically strove to beat down the Kandhs to the level of helpless drudges.[35]

Chintamani Nanda, the Tahsildar of Kandhamals[35a] under the Bengal administration, pleaded with him for a better deal with the Kandhs only to be sternly told by Udit Pratap that the Kandhs were "a dangerous, treacherous and lazy tribe" who deserved to be reduced to "mere instruments of labour of no more account than so many ploughs of the field."[36]

The Kandhs intensely feared and hated the *kultas* as the very embodiment of systematic oppression. What added insult to injury was the *kulta* treatment of the Kandhs as an inferior people; the *kulta* oppression had, in fact, been institutionalised into a system called *ghoti* under which the heavily indebted Kandh peasant became in course of time the bonded slave of the *kulta* money lender. The *kulta,* while buying from the Kandh, insisted on a bigger measure than what he would accept while selling his wares to the Kandh buyer.[37]

Even in Kutiya Kandh hill tracts Udit Pratap made village-wise settlements, which originally light, were, during the last years of his rule, "unduly enhanced."[38] The Chief did not deal with these wild men directly, but through a class of men called *bissis,* most of whom were Oriya *paiks.* The men exercised considerable influence on the tribesmen.[39]

Udit Pratap at the end of his rule in 1881 had become the richest and the most powerful feudatory chief in the Chattisgarh Agency, the annual revenue of his state having increased five-fold since he had assumed power in 1853.[40] During the years the Kandh peasants had sunk progressively lower in poverty and degradation, being left with "little more than the scant cloth which concealed their nakedness,"[41] and an anguished memory of being the original lords of all their eyes surveyed, the ruling dynasty itself being the creation of their ancestors.

Udit Pratap, "a good Urdu and Oriya scholar", enjoyed the trust of the British government for the particular reason that he had banned the public performance of human sacrifice in the Kandh tracts of his state besides rendering assistance to the Government in dealing with the rebellion of Chakra Bissoyi and the disturbances in the neighbouring Patna state.[42] He had himself tackled Kandh peasant discontent in the Rampur-Madanpur zamindari of his state in 1878. The local zamindar, Harihar Singh was personally not oppressive, but his apathy to administration led his subordinates to oppress the Kandhs. The revenue demand was increased by one hundred per cent, tribal lands were taken possession of by Oriya oil men, the Kandhs were fined for felling trees and selling some forest product. The zamindar's *paiks'* exactions and the molestation of tribal women were the immediate causes of Kandh disturbance. Besides plundering Oriya property, the enraged tribals burnt thirty one villages and killed some men of the zamindar. The Kandhs invited fellow tribals of the neighbouring Patna state in their looting spree. Udit Pratap dealt with the situation both tactfully and firmly, the Deputy Commissioner of Chattisgarh Agency lending him the fullest support. While the state police punished some Kandhs heavily, the Chief conciliated some Kandh leaders. The zamindar, Harihar Singh, had died in the meanwhile, and then Udit Pratap weeded out some bad men from the local administration.[42a]

The death of the masterful Udit Pratap in 1881 led to a scramble for power in the state, the rival pretenders seeking Kandh support to press their claim. The British government promptly recognised an eight-year old adopted son of the deceased Chief, Raghukishore Deo by name. The boy *raja* underwent no customary tribal investiture ceremony; so in Kandh eyes the new rule lacked legitimacy. The Government set aside the claim of an older adopted son of Udit Pratap, by name Ram Bhadra Sai. The Government asked the wife of Udit Pratap to manage the state during the new Chief's minority; the all powerful *dewan,* Sadasiv Nanda, would assist the queen. Ram Bhadra's bitterness further increased when the Government removed him to Raipur, the headquarters of the Chattisgarh Divisional Commissioner. His wife vainly appealed to leading members of the local Oriya landed gentry to espouse the cause of her husband. The dowager queen herself was dissatisfied with the Government's decision, for she wanted her daughter's son to be recognised as the new Chief of the state.[43]

The Kandhs took the fullest opportunity of the unsettled affairs of the Court to impress on the British government that their accumulated grievances be redressed. They were particularly sore with the overassessment of their lands, exaction of cesses by state officers, the extinction of the traditional rights of the *Umraos* and the systematic alienation of tribal lands to *kultas*. For eight months after the death of Udit Pratap the Kandh peasants kept appealing to all the British officers concerned with the administration of Kalahandi—the Deputy Commissioner of Sambalpur, Assistant Commissioner of Raipur and, finally, the Chief Commissioner of the Central Provinces himself during his tour of Raipur. When all appeals failed, the Kandh peasants withheld the payment of land tax to the Kalahandi state.[44]

Ram Bhadra Sai, the pretender, met Kandh *sardars* at Raipur and assured them that he would get all their grievances redressed and the land tax, in particular, reduced, if they pressed the British government to make him the Chief of the state.[45]

In January 1882, reports reached the Government of Kandh peasants having plundered 142 villages in the Kalahandi *khalsa* held by rich Oriya farmers.[46]

That the event caught the Government completely unawares established its total lack of touch with the realities of the local tribal life. The annual reports on the state in the few preceding years contained nothing about the brewing discontent among the Kandh peasantry, let alone about the impending uprising. The Commissioner's tour through the Kandh tract as late as February 1882 was just a routine affair; he claimed to have received no complaint whatever from any Kandh peasant. The only explanation which the Commissioner, Lucie Smith, could find for this was the great dread in which the Kandhs held Udit Pratap and his *dewan*, and their conviction that since they enjoyed the Government's confidence, no complaint against them would ever be entertained by the Government.[47] Above all, as Lucie Smith confessed himself :

> The measures which produced the discontent produced all the material prosperity of the country, and the short time which the civil authorities could occasionally pass in Kalahandi gave them no chance of discovering the evils which lay beneath the fair-seeming surface.[48]

What particularly established the short sightedness of the local authorities was the fact that the tribal peasantry in several parts of the province were an unhappy lot, and there had been uprisings in some feudatory states in the province just a few years ago.[49] In fact, the authorities were not ignorant of the general problem of the local tribal peasantry; they were rather indifferent, and that created the crisis situation in Kalahandi.

The plunder of *kulta* villages stung the Government to action. Lucie Smith himself made an on-the-spot enquiry and found the state in utter confusion with revenue not collected and many defaulters jailed. He pacified the enraged Kandh peasants by persuasion and a show of force, bringing in troops and police parties. But then, he was convinced of the genuineness of the Kandh grievance. Indeed,

> for years past they, in common with the rest of the population of the Khalsa, have lived under a rule of systematic injustice which placed the rights and liberty of everyone in the state at the mercy of intriguing and unscrupulous officials.[50]

They had not dared appealing to British officers for fear of reprisal by the all powerful *dewan.* It rather surprised the Commissioner that despite such prolonged oppression, the Kandhs had so long refrained from any physical violence to their tormentors.[50a] In such circumstances Lucie Smith wanted that the Kandhs be treated leniently by the Government and that a general amnesty be declared after the Kandhs returned the looted *kulta* property.[51]

He assured the Kandhs that the Government would conduct a full enquiry into all the tribal grievances and the land revenue demand would be reduced if the enquiry established that it was indeed excessive. Lucie Smith wanted a new land settlement to be conducted by F.C. Berry, Assistant Secretary to the Chief Commissioner, who would take prominent Kandh *majhis* into confidence in doing his job.[52]

Lucie Smith was convinced that the only arrangement, which was just in itself and likely to pacify the tribals, was to acknowledge the rights of Kandh peasants in some form over all the villages originally founded by their ancestors, to abolish all the objectionable cesses and imposts, to reduce the land revenue demand, liquor and *pandhari* assessment[53] wherever they were unduly heavy. Smith did not want to weaken the authority of either the Kalahandi Chief or his Oriya underlings on the tribal peasantry; he would only prevent the authority to be palpably misused for wantonly exploiting the Kandhs. The Chief would continue to rule the tribals; only the Government, unlike heretofore, would closely oversee his administration.

In fact, the Commissioner was all for accommodating the apparently conflicting interests of the Kandhs and *kultas,* recognising the one's traditional rights and the other's contribution to the agricultural development of the state. The Kandh claim to receiving justice was as strong as the Government's own interest in the increasing revenue of the state through the agency of the enterprising Oriya farmers. This was the basis of the settlement which Lucie Smith effected at a place called Arjai; local Oriya zamindars and Kandh *sardars* approved of the settlement. The Arjai settlement provided that :

(a) When a village was presently held by a non-Kandh *gaontia* for less than twelve years, it should be restored to the representative of the original Kandh *majhi* of the village.

(b) If a tank had been constructed or new ground made fit for cultivation in the above village by the present non-Kandh *gaontia* at his own expense, be would continue to hold the land but only as a ryot in the village.

(c) Each non-Kandh *gaontia* so ousted would be given waste lands to enable him to found a village. The lands would be held by him rent-free for five years; then they would be assessed; he would not be evicted as long as he paid the rent.

(d) When a non-Kandh *gaontia* had held a village for more than twelve years, he would be retained as a *gaontia,* but the representative of the original Kandh *majhi* would be given a plot of cultivable land in the village which would be rent free; he would also be given half of the village waste land.[54]

Lucie Smith held it inexpedient to recognise the *Umraos* as heads of circles of villages, for "to do this would be to restore an unnecessary and possibly a dangerous body of men between the Chief and the *majhis,*[55] but the Commissioner would at the same time attach the surviving members of the old *Umraos* families to the Government by giving them some revenue-free lands and reduced *Jumma* . However , in the very special cases, he would recognise those as *Umraos* whose relatives had held the position during the rule of Udit Pratap, the recognition being conditional on the men having done the Government some service in tackling the Kandh discontent, the current problem.[56] Since the *paiks* were an "important class", Lucie Smith would keep them in good humour by assuring them that he would enquire into their complaint that their rent-free lands had been assessed by the late Chief.[57] Smith's policy was conciliatory as further evidenced by his restoring the authority of several prominent *majhis* and reinstating some others in the villages from where they had been ousted by the local *kultas.*[58]

Lucie Smith knew that the immediate result of the Arjai settlement would be some reduction in the state revenue, but he has hopeful that very soon the loss would be made up by the extension of cultivation effected by a contented tribal peasantry. In fact, the land in Kalahandi was extremely fertile, being well-watered; failure of crops due to drought was rather unknown, and was "likely to remain unknown".[59] Further, since the state was connected with Bombay, Raipur and the eastern sea coast, a flourishing trade could grow there.[60]

The Commissioner wanted to form a distinct Kandh district with Kalahandi and the neighbouring states, Khariar, Borasamber and Patna, all populated by tribals, in it, and with Bhawanipatna as its headquarters. In fact, in 1856, Captain Elliot, the Commissioner of Chattisgarh, had proposed such a measure which, in spite of the approval of the Commissioner of Nagpur, could not be implemented on account of the outbreak of the revolt of 1857.[61]

Lucie Smith viewed the short-lived Kandh outbreak as but a natural reaction to the prolonged oppression the men had suffered; the Kandh peasantry, he was convinced, was generally well-affected towards the British government and was peace-loving. Some Kandhs, in the Commissioner's presence,[62] restored to the *kultas* their looted property, confirming his belief of having effected a peaceful termination of the disturbance.

That the Commissioner had rather misjudged the situation became clear when only a few days before he left Kalahandi, reports of renewed disturbance reached him. The "every sign of quiet" that he had seen after the Arjai settlement turned out to be the proverbial lull before the storm. Nearly 350 villages spread over 400 square miles of territory were involved in the second phase of the disturbance. While plundering the *kulta* property was the only motive of the first phase of the tribal uprising, physical destruction of the *kultas* was the apparent object of the second. In fifty villages, particularly, the massacre of *kultas,* men, women and children, was extensive and ruthless, mutilation of limbs preceding their execution.[63] There were even reports of the revival of the rite of human sacrifice. The Kandhs sent bent arrows and heads of murdered *kultas* to neighbouring tribal tracts seeking their support. The Kandhs of Jeypore, who had no apparent grievance against the *kultas,* also joined the fray.[64]

This was the situation in Kandh tracts of Kalahandi when F. C. Berry took over charge as the Superintendent of Kalahandi affairs. Berry had a two fold task : to firmly put down the uprising, and then to redress the just grievances of the Kandh peasantry by a new settlement which differed in some respects from Lucie Smith's settlement at Arjai. Berry rose equal to the occasion. First, he organised a swift but small campaign, and thereby inflicted exemplary punishment to Kandh leaders to terrorise them. Troops were brought from Raipur, Sambalpur, Berhampur, Nagpur, Bhandara and Bilaspur, and soon the Kandh desperadoes were flushed out of their hideouts. Berry executed some Kandh leaders without the orders of the Chief Commissioner, got some others mercilessly flogged and set some villages afire—severe measures for which the C.P. Government was later pulled up by the Government of India.[65] Berry disarmed the Kandh peasants who lived in the *khalsa;* they were only allowed to retain their bows and arrows under license,[66] they being needed to keep away animals and birds from standing crops. Greatly scared, the Kandhs submitted to the Government; the uprising was quelled.

The second uprising Berry attributed to Smith's conciliatory measures, particularly his misplaced clemency towards Kandh *sardars* who had looted the *kulta* property; the men, according to Berry, deserved no lenient treatment. In fact, Berry's enquiry established that for long after they had agreed to the Arjai settlement, they had not returned most of the looted *kulta* property; they had viewed Smith's leniency as the Government's weakness and fear. The Kandh-*kulta* ill feelings were far more deep rooted than Smith had supposed, for nothing short of the expulsion of the *kultas* farm the Kalahandi state, lock, stock and barrel, and the immediate revival of the powers of the *Umraos* would pacify the Kandhs.[67] And neither would be conceded by Berry who favoured a strong arm policy to deal with the Kandhs.

From the very outset Berry found the implementation of all the proposals of Smith not only difficult but undesirable. He would in no case review the practically extinct powers of the *Umraos* though fully utilising their influence with the Kandhs to pacify them. For even a limited revival of the *Umraos'* position, as recommended by Smith, would result in the reinforcement of their traditional authority on the Kandh peasantry without bringing the latter under secure control of the Government. Smith's scheme of distributing to Kandh peasants waste lands also seemed impracticable, for such lands hardly existed.[68]

But then, like Smith, Berry's general policy was also to adjust the conflicting relations of the Kandh peasants and *kultas,* so that the extension of cultivation through the agency of the latter continued unabated while the former's general condition did not further deteriorate as a result. In the agrarian economy of the state the *kultas* had brought about a great change, and so to drive them away, as demanded by the Kandhs, would result in throwing the "country back in civilisation half a century."[69]

Hence, Berry would not even return to their original Kandh owners the lands held by the *kultas,* for thereby the land revenue of the state would decrease—the Kandh, peasants, according to Berry, being thriftless, indolent and unenterprising. The Government could hardly ignore the fact that before the Kandh lands were expropriated by the *kultas,* the Kandh peasants had been unable to pay even the nominal revenue demand at that time. In contrast, the hardworking *kultas,* having occupied the lands, increased their productivity so much as to justify a much enhanced revenue demand by the state.[70]

Berry made the village the basis of his new settlement, and not the *desh.* The settlement was to be made for three years with individual ryots who would remit their respective dues to the local *gaontia.* The *gaontia* was recognised as just a leaseholder for the period of the settlement with no proprietary right to the village. In return for his service as the collector of the Government's revenue demand, he would get a piece of rent-free land. Two other village officers, the *jhankar,* who performed the worship of the village deity, and *gonda,* the village watchman, would also get rent-free land.[71]

Berry was cautious in dealing with the wild Kutiya Kandhs, whom he had succeeded in holding back from joining the fray. He would reward some Kutiya leaders whom he personally knew for having maintained peace in their tracts despite the temptations and inducements offered by the rebel Kandhs. He lessened the Government's revenue demand from the Kutiya territory, substituting payment in kind by payment in cash. He recognised the *bissimajhis* as the communication link between the tribesmen and the Government when the men made it clear that they wanted no replacement of the *bissimajhis,* although they were oppressive at times.[72]

To conciliate the Kandhs, Berry restored tribal headmanship of several villages, persuading the local *kultas* to retain their holdings as tenants. The affluent *kulta* tenants would now pay their rents to the newly recognised Kandh headmen, now called *gaontias.*[73] The Government sought to attach the new Kandh *gaontias* to itself, they being made individually responsible for the remittance of land revenue by their respective villages.

The Kalahandi Kandh uprising brought out the inadequacy of the local police establishment. The police were in a state of sullen discontent over long arrears of pay; not unoften were they hand in gloves with the local law breakers.[74] Berry took a critical look at the *paik* establishment, so long viewed as an essential element in tribal administration. The role of the *paiks* in the uprising had really been far from helpful to the Government; Berry was convinced of the men's deliberate inaction at some places and covert complicity with the tribals in the spoliation of the *kultas* at some others. And still, as a deliberate measure of conciliation, the Government did not abolish the *paik* establishment altogether; the men were retained in service with reduced responsibility, power and privilege. They would now function as auxiliaries of the police under leaders of proven loyalty to the Government; their traditionally rent-free service holdings would now be subject to a light rent.[75] The police outposts were new increased in number both as a security measure and as a "civilising influence". The government of the Central Provinces would defray half the cost of the enlarged police establishment, the other half being borne by the Kalahandi state.[76]

The uprising also made it clear to the Government that the only guarantee against the continued misgovernment in a feudatory state was the assumption of the local administration by the British government itself. And this was promptly done, Berry being appointed the Administrator.[77]

The peasant uprising in Kalahandi was the culmination of the pent-up discontent in the Kandh tract of which the C. P. government had some knowledge, but of the gravity of which it had no adequate appreciation. The uprising was not so much against the British government as against the Kalahandi Chief's prolonged misrule in general and the economic deprivation of the tribal peasantry caused by the affluent Oriya farmers in particular.

The uprising highlighted the inconsistency between the traditional position of the tribal peasantry in the economic life of the state and the acquired authority of non-tribals in it—a fact so long overlooked by the British government. The problem now was how to resolve the inconsistency without suddenly changing the existing situation. Peace in the Kalahandi tribal tracts would now depend largely on the effectiveness of the measures to control the non-tribal propensity to exploit the tribals. In fact, the developing conflict of interests between the tribal and the Oriya peasantry lay in the very logic of circumstances—a fact of which the British government was really not wholly unaware. It did have the knowledge of the basic land problem which had caused small uprisings among Kandh peasants of some neighbouring feudatory states in the previous decade itself.[78]

The Government hoped that the uprising would leave a salutary lesson on both the Kandhs and *Kultas,* and willy nilly they would live peacefully. The *kultas,* so the Government hoped, would refrain from driving the Kandhs to desperation while the fear of stern reprisal by the Government would restrain the Kandhs from wreaking vengeance on the *kultas.* Both would now seek the British government's mediation to adjust their conflicting relations.

The Government now realised as never before the importance of the Oriya zamindars in the Kalahandi state. But for the control of these zamindars over the Kandhs, the disturbance would have been far wider and far more difficult to quell. This was particularly so in respect of the Kutiya Kandh tracts where the local Oriya aristocracy wielded great influence. No wonder, hereafter, the "cardinal point" in the administration of the tribal tracts was "to uphold the authority of the zamindars in their respective tracts and through them to maintain touch with the Kutia Kandhs."[79]

Not all the British officers who dealt with the crisis looked at the problem of Kandh discontent the same way nor did they hold the same opinion on how to address it. While Ismay[80] and Lucie Smith were convinced of the genuineness of the tribal grievances, Ward[81] and Berry blamed the Kandhs for wilful over-reaction to the oppressive state administration. The former two officers would deal sympathetically with the aggrieved tribals, while the latter ones would mete out exemplary punishment to them.

Berry and Ward found little basis in the Kandh allegation of land grabbing by the *kultas,* for there were still arable lands enough for double the existing population of the state. It appeared to them that the Kandhs were intensely jealous of the *kultas,* whose flourishing lands they craved on the plea that they were the original owners of all the lands and that outsiders had no right to any land whatever. In fact, while the Kandh lands looked "slovenly and neglected", *kulta* lands were just the reverse, with "fields well bunded, no opportunity of irrigation lost, groves planted and every sign of industrious labour". The Kandh peasant was thus "not so much a patriot as a plunderer."[82]

However, it would appear that Ward and Berry's estimate of the Kandh character was biased and unfair. The same people in the neighbouring Patna state, which was under the management of the Government, turned out to be prosperous cultivators who had brought new lands under tillage and constructed bunds to irrigate them.[83] Besides, the Kalahandi Kandhs could scarcely ignore the fact that while their brethren in the neighbouring Chinnakimedi Agency tracts and the Kandhmals enjoyed rent-free land, they had to bear a crushing land tax and the unabated dispossession of their ancestral lands by non-tribals.[84]

In fact, the Kandh peasants were not necessarily a troublesome people; only prolonged misrule and grave provocation made them so. Thanks to the direct administration of tribal tracts in Boud, Chinnakimedi and the Patna state, the local Kandhs had become peaceable, loyal and enterprising people as reported by local officers themselves. It was the interposition of the autocratic administration in a feudatory state between the paramount British power and the local tribal population which explained much of the latter's misery.

It was also significant that although the Kalahandi administration had spared no means of beating down the Kandhs "to the level of helpless drudges", it had failed to extinguish their spirit. Ismay found the Kandhs having kept up –

> their passionate belief that they are the masters of the soil, their organisation is still complete, their country is still divided into original Kandh *deshas,* the clans of the several *deshas* are still distinct, and the influence of the Umraos, although

weakened, is still great.[85]

A long period of oppression had only intensified their common feeling of deprivation; and it was this feeling which had held the Kandhs together during the uprising.

The Kandh strength lay in their system of organised life, their absolute loyalty to leaders, their system of secret intelligence and their ability to quickly collect in large tribal bodies at the call of their leaders who held an absolute sway on the rank and file. There was during the uprising no case of desertion or betrayal of leaders; instead, the Kandhs were convinced that their cause was just and no reprisal was too severe to influence them to abandon it.

The revolt left one more lesson for the Government : feudatory states with a large tribal population in them needed to be more effectively controlled by the paramount power than they had been hitherto, for the discontent among the tribal peasantry in the plains could spread to their kinsmen in the hills where the hold of the Chiefs and the British government was far less secure; an armed revolt by the hill tribals could pose greater problem.

One dimension of the tribal problem of which the Government needed to be careful was the direct relation between tribal discontent and dissensions and scramble for power among members of the ruling family of feudatory states. Pretenders for power often set their tribal followers against the British government as a pressure tactics. This obliged the Government not only to intervene in the familial quarrels in the ruling family of feudatory states but also to enter into closer relations with the local tribal leaders as a means of generating confidence in their followers. The Government made the fullest use of the strong community spirit in the tribal society; it kept the *majhis* in good humour, the men being rewarded for their services to the local administration. As for the Chief of the feudatory state, his traditional right to manage his tribal subjects through Oriya zamindars and their hirelings would not be taken away by the British government, but the Chief's ultimate responsibility for better administration of his tribal tracts was forcefully asserted by the paramount power on each occasion when the tracts were afflicted with law and order problem.

Notes and References

1. The Rampas of East Godavari District in the Madras Presidency and the tribals of the Bastar state in the Central Provinces rose in armed revolt in 1878 and 1876 respectively.
2. Most of western Orissa, with a large number of princely states in it, were vassals of the Bhonsles of Nagpur. In 1818, following the defeat of the Bhonsles by the British in the third Maratha war, these states became the tributaries of the British government.

2a. Letters from the Chief Commissioner, Central Provinces, to Govt. of India 1868 (available in Madhya Pradesh Secretariat Record Room, Nagpur)—hereafter cites as MPSRO) : Officiating Deputy Commissioner, Sambalpur to Commissioner, Chattisgarh Division, Raipur, 17 Mar. 1868.

3. Letters from the Chief Commissioner, Central Provinces to the Govt. of India, No. 985, 1868 : Asst. Secretary to the Chief Commissioner to the Secretary, Govt. of India, Foreign Deptt., 30 Mar. 1868.

3a. Tribal leaders also received from the ruler on such occasions some presents in return.

4. Letters to the Govt. of India, 1868 : Officiating Deputy Commissioner, Sambalpur to Commissioner, Chattisgarh Division, 17 Mar. 1868. Sambalpur, a princely state in western Orissa lapsed to the British government in 1849, the ruler having died with no male heir to succeed him. Surendra Sai, a scion of the ruling family, raised the standard of revolt in 1857-58, taking advantage of the "Mutiny" then raging in many parts of India. He was apprehended and kept imprisoned in Asirgarh fort till 1884, when he died there, aged ninety.
5. Officiating Deputy Commissioner, Sambalpur to Commissioner, Chattisgarh Division, 17 Mar. 1868, *op. cit.*
6. *Ibid.*
7. *Ibid.*
8. Asst. Secretary to Chief Commissioner to Secretary, Govt. of India, Foreign Deptt., 30 Mar. 1868, *op. cit.*
9. *Ibid.*
10. Officiating Deputy Commissioner, Sambalpur to Commissioner, Chattisgarh Division, 19 March, 1868.
11. *Ibid.*
12. Letters from the Chief Commissioner to the Govt. of India, No. 985, 1868 : Minute of the Chief Commissioner, 25 Mar. 1868.

12a. *Ibid.*

13. Letters from the Chief Commissioner to Govt. of India, No. 1618/162, 1868 : Secretary to Chief Commissioner to Secretary, Govt. of India, Foreign Deptt., 22 May 1868, forwarding letter from Major A. B. Cumberlege, Deputy

Commissioner, Sambalpur to Commissioner, Chattisgarh Division.

14. Letters from the Chief Commissioner to Govt. of India, No. 2169/191, 1868 : Assistant Secretary to the Chief Commissioner to Secretary, Foreign Dept. 10 July 1868 and its enclosure, Major Cumberlege to Commissioner, Chattisgarh Division, 3 June 1868.
15. *Ibid.*
16. *Ibid.*
17. *Ibid.*
18. Letters from Chief Commissioner to Govt. of India 1870 : Secy. to Chief Commissioner (hereafter CC) to Sec. For. Dept., Govt. of India, 2 Aug. 1870.
19. *Ibid.* 1873 : Report of Captain Bowie on Administration of Patna, 1871-2.
20. Foreign Political Proceedings (hereafter FPP), MPSRO 7, Feb. 1873, Nos. 1-4 : Captain Bowie, Officiating Deputy Commissioner, Sambalpur, to Commissioner, Chattisgarh Division, 8 Aug. 1872.
21. Letters of the CC to Govt. of India, 1874 : Bowie to Commissioner, Chattisgarh, 4 Dec. 1874.
22. *Ibid.:* J. W. Neill, Offg. Secy. to CC, to Commissioner, Chattisgarh, 4 Dec. 1874.
23. *Ibid.,* 1872 : Bowie to Commissioner, Chattisgarh, 22 July 1871.
24. *Ibid.,* 1872 : Bowie to Commissioner, Chattisgarh, 15 July 1870; Secy. to CC to Secy. For. Deptt., Govt. of India, 2 Aug. 1870.
25. *Ibid.,* Bowie to Commissioner, Chattisgarh, 15 July 1870; Secy. to CC to Secy. For. Deptt., Govt. of India, 2 Aug. 1870
26. Foreign Political A Proceedings, NAI, 2 Jan. 1882, No. 2
27. The five zamindaries were Lanjigarh, Karlapath, Thuamul, Kasipur and Mohan Patna, All The zamindars were Oriyas.
28. FPA, 2 Jan. 1882, No. 2 : Lucie Smith to Secy. to CC, 22 May 1882. FPA, 3 Mar. 1882, No. 2 : Berry, Political Agent, Kalahandi, to Secy. to CC, 15 Jan. 1884.
29. *Ibid.:* Lucie Smith to Secy. to CC, 22 May 1882, *op. cit.*
30. Udit Pratap Deo is named as Uditnarayan Deb in some records.
31. FPA, 1 Mar. 1884, No. 7 : Memorandum on Kalahandi affairs by W. B. Jones, CC.
32. FPA, 2 Jan. 1882, No. 2 : Lucie Smith to Secy, to CC, 22 May 1882.
33. *Ibid.*
34. *Ibid.*
35. *Ibid.* FPA, 3 March 1884, No. 2, Berry to Commissioner, Chattisgarh, 15 Jan. 1884.

35a. Kandhmal (or Khondmal as in official records) was a Kandh tract in the district of Angul under the Bengal administration. Before 1855, this tract was under the direct rule of the *raja* of Angul.

36. FPA, 2 Jan. 1882, No. 2, Lucie Smith to Secy. to CC, 22 May 1882. Also Berry's Report, 15 Jan. 1884, *op. cit.*

37. Lucie Smith to Secretary to CC, 22 May 1882, *op. cit.*

38. Berry's Report, *op. cit.*

39. *Ibid.*

40. In 1856 his revenue demand was Rs. 22,387; in 1881 it was 1,27,517 rupees. Lucie Smith to Secretary to CC, 22 May 1882, *op. cit.*

41. *Ibid.*

42. See pp. 14, 36, 91-93 before.

42a. FPA, 2 Apr. 1878, Nos. 1-4.

43. Letters from the Govt. of India, Foreign Deptt. to the CC, MPSRO, 1882 : H. C. Ward, Additional Commissioner, Kalahandi Affairs to Secy. to CC, 1 Aug. 1882.

44. *Ibid.* : A. H. L. Fraser, Officiating Secy. to CC to Secy. For. Deptt., Govt. of India, 11 Sept. 1882. *Ibid.* : Ward to Secy. to CC, 1 Aug. 1882; *Ibid.* : Berry's Report, *op. cit.*

45. *Ibid.* : Ward to Secy. to CC, 1 Aug. 1882, *op. cit.*

46. *Ibid.* : Lucie Smith to Secy. to CC, 8 Mar. 1882.

47. Berry's Report, *op. cit.* FPA, 2 Jan. 1882, No.2: Lucie Smith to Secy. to CC, 31 May 1882.

48. *Ibid.*

49. In 1876, there was a widespread tribal uprising in Bastar state. In Bamra there was a Kandh uprising in 1868. In the neighbouring state of Patna, the Kandhs had revolted shortly thereafter. In Rampur-Madanpur zamindari in the Kalahandi state itself there had been a Kandh uprising in 1878-9.

50. Letters from the Chief Commissioner to the Govt. of India, 1882 : Lucie Smith to Secy. to CC, 20 Feb. 1882.

50a. *Ibid.*

51. *Ibid.* : Secy. to CC to Commissioner, Chattisgarh, Jan. 1882.

52. *Ibid.* Secy. to CC to Secy. Foreign Deptt. Govt. of India, 8 Mar. 1882.

53. FPA, 2 Jan. 1882, No. 2 : Lucie Smith to Secy. to CC, 22 May 1882. FPA, 3 Mar. 1884, No. 2 : Berry to Commissioner, Chattisgarh, 15 Jan. 1884.

54. Lucie Smith to Secy. to CC, 22 May 1882, *op. cit*

55. *Ibid.*

56. *Ibid.*

57. *Ibid.*

58. *Ibid.* Lucie Smith also banned the existing practice of engaging tribal *coolies* to carry the baggages of officers on duty and giving them no payment at all. Officers were also prohibited from demanding free supplies of provisions from

the tribal peasants.

59. FPA, 1 Mar. 1884 : Fraser to Commissioner, Chattisgarh, 1 Mar. 1884.
60. *Ibid.* , 2 Jan. 1882, No. 2 : Lucie Smith to Secy. to CC, 22 May 1882.
61. *Ibid.*
62. Letters from the CC to Govt. of India, 1882 : Fraser to Secy. For. Deptt., Govt. of India, 11 Sept. 1882.
63. *Ibid.* Same to same, 10 June 1882, 24 June 1882, Ward to Secy. to CC, 16 June 1882. FPA, 1 Mar. 1884, No. 6: Ward to Secy. to CC, 18 Sept. 1883.
65. Letters from CC to Govt. of India, 1882 : Berry to Ward, 15 June 1882.
65. *Ibid.* Fraser to Secy. to CC, 16 Aug. 1882.
66. *Ibid.* Ward to Secy. to CC, 20 July 1882.
67. *Ibid.* Fraster to Secy. For. Deptt., Govt. of India, 11 Sept. 1882.
68. FPA, 11 Sept. 1882, No. 3: Berry to Ward, 27 July 1882.
69. FPA, 11 Sept. 1882, No. 9: Fraser to Ward, 11 Sept. 1882. Berry's Report, 27 July 1882, *op. cit.*
70. *Ibid.*
71. FPA, 3 Mar. 1884, No. 2 : Berry to Commissioner, Chattisgarh, 15 Jan. 1884. Earlier in purely Kandh villages the *gaontia* did not own any *bhogra* or rent-free land.
72. *Ibid.*
73. *Ibid.*
74. FPA, 2 Jan. 1882, No. 2: Lucie Smith to Secy. to CC, 22 May 1882.
75. Letters from CC to Govt. of India, 1882 : Ward to Secy. to CC, 20 July 1882.
76. *Ibid.* Fraser to Ward, 11 Sept. 1882.
77. *Ibid.* : Fraser to Secy. For. Deptt. Govt. of India, 11 Sept. 1882.
78. See pp. 91-93 above.
79. FPA, 1 March 1884, No. 7: Memorandum by W. B. Jones, CC, on the affairs of the Kalahandi state.
80. Ismay was Asst. Commissioner, Kalahandi.
81. Col. H. C. Ward was Asst. Commissioner, Kalahandi.
82. Letter from CC to Govt. of India, 1882 : Ward to Secy. to CC, 1 Aug. 1882.
83. FPA, 2 Jan. 1882, No. 2 : Lucie Smith to Secy. to CC, 22 May 1882.
84. *Ibid.*
85. *Ibid.*

9

Tribal Administration in Transition : The Ganjam Agency, 1935-1947

The main problem of an administration in transition is the one of adjustment between the wisdom of conserving tradition and the urgency of changing the accustomed set up. Caution is the keynote of the administration while taking any bold initiative is considered risky. There are no-changers and pro-changers in the administration, who ultimately settle for a compromise. In the end, change is effected no doubt, but its pace is carefully regulated; the administrator does forge forward but with steps, halting and hesitant. He is at times deterred by the experiences of his predecessors while not being very sure if his own steps were the right ones to take. He recognises the need to change his own mindset, but feels indecisive regarding the scope and scale of the change he is to bring about in the life of the people under his charge. All this was clear in the administration of the Ganjam Agency in the last decade of the British rule there.

In December 1938, the Congress ministry in Orissa appointed a committee to enquire into the problems of the tribal tracts of the province, which, under the Government of India Act, 1935, had been declared "Partially Administered Areas" being beyond the pale of general administration of the province. The provision of franchise in the Act did not apply to the tribal areas, the local people being treated by the Government as its protected wards who had better be kept away from the turbulent political currents then sweeping the regularly administered areas of the province.

A little more than a decade later, when the British rule in India ended, the tribal tracts were brought under regular administration, the local people drawn into the new political process based on universal adult suffrage and participative government. For the Government this rather sudden political change in the situation posed a difficult administrative problem; for the local people the problem was one of adaptation to unaccustomed political forces.

By 1938, the tribal life in the Ganjam Agency had indeed changed, the result of both administrative policy and force of circumstances. The British government recognised the change, while admitting that it had at places taken an unintended, and even undesirable, course. Local officers, for their part, admitted the inadequacy and even inefficacy of some current measures. The tribals, still quiescent and unable to strongly react to measures harming their life needed protection against exploitation by those very instruments of administration which the Government had so long been using for changing the moral and material life of the tribals. Thus, the Oriya elite as much as the subordinate staff of the local administration had to be restrained to allay the grievances of the tribals.

The Government clearly saw that administrative measures had changed the relationship between the tribals and non-tribals of the Ganjam Agency, mostly to the detriment of the former, and the latter making the most of the measures to strengthen their position in the local life. The traditional inter-dependent relationship between the Oriya elite and the aboriginals had been replaced by a patently dominant-subordinate relationship between the two. Concomitantly, there had been going on a new power adjustment between the members of the Oriya elite themselves.

For the Government it was rather late in the day to stem the process, let alone reverse its course. All that could be done now was to repair some glaring damages to tribal life and to prevent it from worsening further. Since the Madras administration was soon to leave the Ganjam district to the care of the Orissa government,[1] it decided to take no bold step to improve the tribal administration in the district. Finally, the British rule in India ended soon, and hence the reluctance of the Government of Orissa to adopt any strikingly new aboriginal policy either.

Thus the Orissa government after 1947 inherited a system of tribal administration in Ganjam, of the defects of which it was fully conscious, but which could neither be replaced forthwith by a new one nor retained in tact, for either course would hurt tribal interests. The new administrators naturally observed for some years the old accustomed spirit of tribal administration : hasten slowly. The world around, however, was changing very fast.

In the 1930s, the crux of the problem of the Ganjam Agency was the one of the reconciliation of the conflicting interests of the Oriya elite and the local aboriginals; the aboriginals had to be protected against the Oriya elite's oppression without impairing in the process the elite's established influence on tribal life. For the Government the elite constituted the most dependable means of governance of the tribal tracts by proxy. The elite's power and influence had grown in direct proportion to their use by the Government as the most effective channel of change in tribal life. Assuming more authority than customary, they disregarded the very basic feature of earlier tribal administration—adherence to tradition and consideration for local feelings and susceptibilities.

This was best evidenced by the frequent disputes over free service (*bethi)* and free gifts (*mamul)* claimed by the Oriya elite and contested by the tribals. The *patros, bissoyis, hoddadars and paiks* grudged what appeared to them as reluctance to meet their traditional obligation, while the tribals resisted what to them was blatant exactions; the occasion for the payment of *mamul* and rendering *bethi* and the number of claimants for both tended to be far more numerous than recognised by tribal custom and tradition.

But then, the increasing disputes over *mamul* and *bethi* were more the symbol of economic maladjustment between the tribals and the Oriya elite than its cause. The cause lay in the process of economic change set in motion by the administration itself. The introduction of money economy in the tribal tracts, the extension of agriculture by the non-tribals in the Agency, the development of communication links, the growth of export and import trade through markets set up by the Government, the increasing immigration and settlement of Oriya traders and money lenders in tribal tracts and the steady exposure of the tracts to the world outside—all this kept widening the economic frontier of the Agency areas, though not bringing in equal measure any economic benefits to the local aboriginals. The men felt being out of step with the changing economic situation, to which the non-tribals adjusted themselves far better. For the Oriya elite, in particular, Agency administration provided expanding economic opportunities; for the tribals it had caused economic deprivation. It was not the declared objective of the administration, it was but its unintended result.

With more forests declared reserved and out of bounds for tribal axe cultivation, and forest products banned for tribal use, the economic misery of the aboriginals deepened. Roads, mostly constructed with tribal labour, took out from the Agency goods far more in volume than the goods they brought in, the process making local products scarcer and dearer. Government restrictions on the customary tribal practice of distilling liquor from *sago* and *mahua* trees, and the sale of cheap liquor through Oriya contractors (*sundhis)* increased drunkenness among the aboriginals rather than curbing it, as intended by the Government. Mortgage and sale of tribal lands to Oriya immigrants was directly related to the growing economic hardship of the aboriginals, which itself was aggravated by their increasing drunkenness. The widening economic gap between the tribals and non-tribals was the fallout of the Agency administration itself, though not its intended object.[2]

Agency officers had a mixed feeling over the growing tribal assertiveness against their tormentors, *patros* and *bissoyis.* It was a good development, indicating the tribals coming of age and their refusal to suffer any longer the oppressive tutelage of the Oriya elite. But then, such tutelage being the corner stone of the tribal administration, its impairment involved the prospect of the Government assuming the direct responsibility of tribal management, this the government was wholly averse to do, considering the difficult terrain and climatic conditions and problems of communication. Tribal complaints against exactions were indeed genuine, but there was also some substance in the grievances of *patros* and *bissoyis* that the measures of the administration had affected their economic interests too. They had to pay the Government the stipulated tribute, though their income had fallen due to many forests having been reserved and many forest products declared as commodities for exclusive use by the Government and for sale by the Government alone.[3]

In such circumstances the Oriya elite found it hard to maintain their accustomed panoply of power, to exact *mamuls* from the tribals as also to discharge their increasing obligations to the local administration. Their *hoddadars* and *paiks* were not as obedient and obliging as before, for the men had tasted power themselves while feathering their own nests by exacting *mamuls* and *bethi* from the tribals; and tradition forbade any interference by *paiks* and *bissoyis* with their retainers' freeholds, all service tenures. Even the extension of cultivation at places by Oriya immigrants and other non-tribal settlers — Telugu farmers, money lenders and liquor contractors—had not benefited the local *patros* and *bissoyis,* because the Government had from time to time set a limit to the kind and quantity of free gifts and the duration and frequency of free service they could claim from the local aboriginals; the Government also banned the imposition of illegal cesses by the Oriya elite. The *bissoyi* of Rayagada had become poor; he had even to mortgage his land to a *pana*—a fact which had compromised his traditional image and position among the local Savaras, and had encouraged their intractability.[4]

The Madras government was fully conscious of these problems in the Ganjam Agency administration; it also knew that the solution lay in the economic uplift of the tribals by comprehensive measures. However, the task was forbidding in point of both time and cost; and so the Government chose to put it off. As before, local officers would keep settling disputes over *mamuls* and *bethi* as and when they occurred, at places pressuring the *patros* and *bissoyis* to scale down their demands and at others persuading the tribals to come to terms with the *muthadars*. Sometimes, oppressive *muthadars* were replaced, and at times tribal prayer for lesser *mamul* and *bethi* was conceded after an enquiry was conducted into the changed economic situation of the tract which justified a lenient attitude to the tribals. Most often the Government temporised, for in the late thirties it had little apprehension of any crisis situation developing out of the deteriorating tribal-non-tribal relationship.

The Government, however, sought to mollify some tribal grievances, the effect of which was to check the exploitative propensities, of the *muthadars*. The latter were now obliged to give receipts for *mamuls* and *bethi*. Savaras of some villages in Parlakhemundi showed local British officers such receipts which they had received many years ago to buttress their argument that the local *muthadar's* latest claim to free gifts and services was far more than customary.[5] This was surely an indicator of the mental maturity of the local tribals. Wide publicity of the acts and regulations to prevent the alienation of tribal lands was another step taken by the Government besides some relaxation of excise rules which permitted tribal manufacture of liquor for home consumption. Forest rules were also amended so that the tribals could use some forest products at home, though not for sale.[6]

As for *bethi*, the Government, after periodical enquiries into the institution in the changing situation and in the context of the changing temper of the tribals, made a compromise between administrative expediency and moral iniquity involved in the issue : extraction of unpaid labour from the tribals was surely unethical, but administratively indispensable, considering the enormous cost involved in executing public works in the Agency. The Government decided to make small payments for hiring tribal labour besides entrusting the Public Works Department with some responsibility for road construction in the Agency for which labourers were paid at a much higher rate than before. At places, Kandhs and Savaras were allowed to commute *bethi* for money, and, at others, *mamuls* could be substituted by payments in cash.[7]

The Government banned the Agency staff demanding from the *muthaheads* free supplies of provisions, for the latter extracted from the tribals much more than they gave the Government employees. The practice of private trading in forest products by the subordinate Agency staff who acted in close concert with local *muthadars* attracted stiff punishment.[8]

However, the Government adopted no uniform policy regarding settlement of disputes on *mamul* and *bethi,* for it recognised that any such policy had to wait till a thorough enquiry was undertaken into the entire gamut of the economic life of the tribals as affected by the Agency administration itself; what added to the problem was the variation in the course and character of the economic change itself between different tracts in the vast Agency, those away from hills and forests having changed much faster, following closer tribal-non-tribal inter-action. The impact of the administration itself varied between regions and so did even the efficacy of the administrative apparatus set up at different places. The rate of *mamuls* and *bethi* fixed by earlier Agency officers was found not quite relevant to the situation in the 1930s, when many villages had been abandoned and many lands lain uncultivated for years, thus reducing the local *muthadars'* income—a fact which the Government did not always take into account while realising its due from them and restraining them from replenishing their income by exacting more from the tribals than fixed by Agency officers years ago. Even where cultivation had extended and the paying capacity of the local tribals had increased, the *muthadars* were restrained from demanding more than what had been recorded as their due in the enquiry report decades ago.[9]

But then, the worst feature of the state of affairs prevalent in the Agency was that, while, in disregard of their worsening economic condition, the tribals were obliged to give *mamuls* and do *bethi* in ever-increasing volume and variety, the thriving Oriya settlers-farmers, *sundhis* and *sowcars*—were free from such obligation.[10] They paid no land tax either, although many tribal lands had passed into their hands. Evidently, they had made the most of the established tradition in the

Agency that none but the native tribals were obliged to give *mamuls* and render *bethi.*[11]

By the late 1930, Agency officers in their reports to the Government freely admitted that most rules and regulations to protect tribal interests had failed dismally, alienation of tribal lands went on unabated, the tribals being either ignorant of the rules to prevent such alienation or too fearful to lodge complaints against the local influential *sundhis* and *sowcars.* The latter often pressurised the tribals to retract their complaints or tempted them with free liquor to disavow their allegations. More absurd was the requirement that charges were to be preferred only through the local *muthadars,* who were themselves many a time charged with mistreatment of the complainants. At times the scared tribal was tutored to confirm the land grabber's plea that the alienation of his land antedated the rules banning it.[12]

Unable to prevent tribal land alienation, the Madras government for a time thought of assessing the lands held by the non-tribals and levying tax on them after bringing them under ryotwari settlement.[12a] Nothing, however, came of this idea, partly because of the enormous cost involved in its execution and partly because of the Government's reluctance to do away with the extant *muthadari* system through which it had so long administered the tribal tracts. It was governance by remote control and with limited liability; the *muthadars* bore the main responsibility of local administration; they functioned as the conduits of the influence of the British government as also local shock absorbers.[13]

The Madras government made no large scale economic reforms in the Ganjam Agency though undertaking some alleviative measures. Cooperative agricultural societies were set up at places and agricultural loans were advanced; new crops were introduced; plantation of fruit bearing trees was encouraged; restrictions on *podu* at some places were relaxed; the police and other subordinate staff were strongly dealt with for mistreating the tribals. Kandhs and Savaras were appointed as watchmen, peons, domestic servants; some were recruited in the local police; some others, the educated ones, were given jobs in schools.

Civilising the tribals remained a mission of the British tribal administration in Orissa till its last days with education being a means to that end. But it was obvious all the while that the real beneficiaries of the Government's educational programme were the non-tribals, not the tribals; increasing number of schools in the tribal tracts was thus no indicator of the level of literacy among the local aboriginals.[13a] The education imparted to the tribals had little relevance to the grim economic realities of tribal life. When immediate economic needs were to be met, distant economic prospects after school education could hardly be a motivating factor for Kandh parents who naturally preferred sending their wards to fields or road construction sites to schools to learn three Rs.. No wonder, the Special Assistant Agent, Baliguda reported to the Agent that when a Kandh child was "released from school, he gladly shook the load of learning off his mind and returned to his original condition".[14] Gift of clothes failed to motivate regular attendance in schools because the children and their parents went about practically naked.[15] Equally ineffective was the persuasion of local officers that a little education would enable the tribals to see through the means by which money lenders deceived them and petition writers in courts fleeced them.[16]

Tribal education was indeed "more ornamental than useful", so the Government admitted in 1934, when an annual investment of a lakh of rupees had produced not even one graduate in the Agency.[17] Parents viewed schools as creches to keep the mischief-making children away from their homes for a few hours. Naturally, therefore, as "the age of children and their economic value increase, there is an increasing reluctance to forego the help they can render for agricultural and pastoral work."[18]

To make the matters worse, those who passed out of schools wanted only teaching jobs; and such jobs were not many.[18a] Official opinion disfavoured expansion of secondary education in the Agency, both the Agent and the Director of Public Instruction wondering if the object of such education was to "transform a perfectly good tribesman into an inefficient clerk."[19] The Government made a modest attempt to set up industrial schools where vocational education was provided to some tribal students. The Government also drew up an order of preference for jobs in the Agency according to caste, not educational attainments, with a view to favouring the Kandhs and Savaras over *panas* and Oriyas.[20]

Social change in the tribal world caused a mixed feeling in the local administrators; acculturation with the non-tribals "civilised" the tribals, but debased their traditional character. Detribalisation was indeed the price paid for the modicum of modernisation brought about by the Government. And this development was noted quite early. In 1884, H. Mounsey, Assistant Agent, saw "a decided improvement in personal cleanliness and a desire to wear clothes purchased from the planes in

Oriya fashion" on the part of the Kandhs who had gone to schools and had interacted with Oriya students there. As for the Kandh girls "they were proud of what they had learnt"; they were eager to display their skill in sewing, in particular.[21] Girls in the Udaygiri market wore bodice which they wove themselves. A few *patros* and *bissoyis* went to colleges. One of them, the *bissoyi* of Gumma, wrote a full-length drama for staging at an official meeting.[22] The Savaras of Sarangada in Parlakhemundi refused to give their customary *mamuls* to the local *bissoyi,* insisting on sending money instead either to the Maharaja of Parlakhemunidi or to the Government by postal money order.[23] All this was indeed a trend to be happy about.

But then, "contact with civilisation" through the local Oriyas changed the Kandh character, making them, for example, far more prone to drunkenness than their fellowmen in the hills where the pace of acculturation with the Oriya had been far slower.[24] Tribal involvement in many court cases, despite the introduction of Stamp Duty as a deterrent, indicated their litigiousness and waning regard for truthfulness; this Agency officers deplored, for the tribals earlier never told a lie.[25] G. F. Padison reported in 1916 on the Kandhs of Ghumsur-Udaygiri having lost much of their traditional traits of character as a result of their closer contact with the people of the plains. In 1933, the Special Assistant Agent, Baliguda found the local Kandhs and Savaras "not the timid and unsophisticated aborigines of the good old days",[25a] and so, unlike before, their deposition could not be relied upon in deciding cases of excess or short collection of *mamuls* by local *muthadheads*. Savaras being no longer as docile as before in their dealings with the *muthaheads* suggested their having "lost their spirit of compromise"; this made the task of local peace keepers difficult.[26]

The process of Hinduisation of the tribals figured frequently in Agency reports. Census figures indicated a large increase of Hindu population in the Agency at the expense of the animists. In 1901, 95.9 per cent of the local people returned themselves as animists; in 1911 the figure fell to 75.1 per cent; in 1921, 82.7 per cent of the local people were animists.[27] The Savaras near Digi in Parlakhemundi were greatly influenced by Hinduism; they supported a Brahmin priest for their religious functions.[28] Car festival was a common celebration of tribals and non-tribals in the southern tracts of the agency, reinforcing the theory of the tribal origin of the national deity of Orissa. *Pano* Christians, the most assertive element in the Agency population, who challenged the *muthadars'* claim to *mumul* and *bethi* the most, gave up eating the flesh of dead animals, their traditional food.[29] There were "Oriyanised Savaras" in Parlakhemundi leading a markedly Hindu way of life.[30] The Gumma *bissoyi* of Parlakhemundi, an educated man, married an illegitimate daughter of the Raja of Surangi[31] — a trans-cultural development. Caste consciousness was not yet evident among the Kandhs, but they viewed the local *panos, dombos* and *gohingas* as far lower in social status.[31a] The Kandh potter, Kandh herdsman and Kandh farmer ate together and inter-married; Kandhs and *panos* drank liquor together, but an offspring of a Kandh-*pano* union had no legitimacy in Kandh society.[32]

Another new social indicator was the Oriya elite's acute sensitivity to their own officially recognised rank and status; in matters of protocol, the rajas, zamindars, *patros* and *bissoyis* reacted the same way as the Oriya aristocracy in non-tribal regions. Periodically meeting these men at regular public ceremony, called *bhet,* was a grand official affair, when Agency officers invested new *patros* and *bissoyis* with their official position, in token whereof, and as a mark of the Government's favour, the men were given scarves, locally called *sadis.* There were some *patros* who got their name painted on their *sadis* to flaunt them before their men as a symbol of their new status.[33] The Government chose these *sadias* for their proven loyalty, wide influence and some education. Agency officers were required to respect the men's feelings about protocol and status. There were a few chiefs high enough in rank to be shaken by their hand, a few *bissoyis* entitled to sit on chairs when visiting Government officers and a few *patros* allowed to sit on carpets or on benches during the *bhet.*[34]

These "Government *Sadias"* created in their turn a class of "private *Sadias",* ceremonially conferring on these men honour and status. The fun and frolic of the *sadi* tying ceremony was a welcome diversion from the monotony of local life, apart from being of some economic significance : on such occasions local *patros* and *paiks* received some gifts from the new *Sadias* and other local dignitaries attending the function.[35] However, the Government was not too happy with the Oriya gentry arrogating to themselves the right to confer titles and honours. Agency officers, in fact, took exception to the chiefs of Ranoba and Korada, two small estates, collecting village taxes from ryots and appointing village officers without any reference to the Government. Being under "the guidance of false superiority", the petty chiefs had been behaving as though they were big zamindars.

Happily for the Government, the Ganjam Agency in the last decade of the British rule was politically not a problem unlike Koraput, Mayurbhanj, Nilgiri, Daspalla, Gangpur and Ranpur, all affected by the Prajamandal movement.[37] An attempt to involve the Savaras of Olanda in Parlakhemundi estate in the Civil Disobedience Movement was successfully dealt with by local authorities[38] who also took measures to prevent any spill-over of Koraput disturbances under Laxman Naik in 1942.[39] The aboriginals of Ganjam had become a peaceable lot, mostly free from the political contagion in non-tribal areas of the province.

Economically too, the Ganjam Agency was not a liability for the Government, inspite of the fact that from most of it, it derived no land revenue at all. The tributes from the local Oriya elite, the sale of sleepers to railway companies and arrack shops to liquor contractors and an export trade in forest products, all this enabled the Government to not only balance the budget but earn a surplus for many years, including the ones during the great depression.[40] The Agency administration also thought of new measures like the leasing of markets in tribal tracts, resumption of lands held by the *paiks* and assessment of tribal lands now owned by non-tribals, all to increase the local earnings.

Tribal migration caused by both economic factors and Government encouragement was another development having social and economic implications. Some Kandhs of Ganjam, prevented from *podu,* migrated to Koraput hills. Labour contractors took many Savaras and Kandhs to Assam tea gardens while, during the first world war, many tribals of Ganjam were taken to Mesopotemia to serve in the labour corps there.[41] The men returned home with some superficial changes in their way of life. They now used soap, hair oil, shoes and cigarettes; their women now preferred aluminium and German silver to traditional kitchenware, goards and earthen pots.[42] Some youngmen, clad in tattered jackets and trousers and smoking cigarettes puffed out some English words—bloody, all right and pussy, for example. They sipped Lipton tea and strutted about with locally made guns slung on their shoulders. Their women, wearing mill made saris and blouses, proudly displayed their imported jewellery, not their traditional heavy brass rings which they had sold for a song to merchants from the plains.[43] Some tribals even gave up beef eating with a view to becoming *bhalajati loka*[44]. Caste feelings showed up among some tribals, whose *panchayats* would fine anyone of the tribe if he was beaten by a *dombo*, an untouchable in Kandh society.[45] Census enumerators came across Kandhs visiting local Hindu temples, patronising Brahmin priests and going on pilgrimages to Hindu shrines, not all very close to their homes.[46] Many Kandhs regarded their acquired fluency in the Oriya language as something to be proud about. In the 1940s, at many places in the Ganjam Agency the popularity of Hindu festivals was as evident as large attendance in traditional tribal religious ceremonies and social festivities.[47]

The tribal world in the Ganjam Agency was changing, but doubts lurked if the change was for the better or worse or whether its pace needed to be accelerated or slowed down. Indian nationalist opinion would encourage closer assimilation of tribal and non-tribal population to quicken the process of emotional—and no less political— integration of the country, while anthropologists, Indian and foreign, opposed it, for it threatened tribal culture and life itself. They were all for the preservation of tribal identity in the face of progressive detribalisation caused by both administrative measures and force of circumstances. As for the tribal administrator, in the last years of the British rule, he recognised the desirability of change in tribal life but not sure either of the pace in which it needed to be brought about or its ultimate object. He knew that the tribals with their life wholly changed would not remain tribals any longer; that raised the question of the continuance of tribal administration at all. No wonder, in such circumstances, the steps the administrator took were all marked by ambivalence—it being the typical characteristic of an administration in transition.

The Partially Excluded Areas Enquiry Committee, composed of Congress legislators and social activists, minced no words when criticising the existing tribal administration in Orissa. The lack of a regular revenue administration, the local peoples' addiction to opium, the "unrestricted and uncompetitive exploitation" of the tribals in the Ganjam and Koraput Agencies, in particular, and the denial of franchise to the tribals came in for critical remarks by the Committee. The yawning economic gap between the tribals and the local Oriyas was commented upon as was the changing economic scenario following unrestricted Oriya immigration and settlement in tribal tracts.[48]

There took place violent clashes between Savaras and *panos* of some tracts in Parlakhemundi following the latter's demand for *mamuls* on behalf of the local *bissoyi.* The Savaras were instigated by the local member of the Orissa Legislative Assembly, himself a *pano,* who had his own personal interests and objects to achieve", but who "externally puts on a garb to show that he is for the uplift of these poor pitiable Savaras."[49] The *panas* setting the Savaras of one *mutha* against those of another was a new development while the police molesting Savara women was indeed a commentary on the local administration itself.[50]

It was in this background that a new view of tribal administration emerged; the tribals, now treated as protected wards of the Government, required help to develop resilience so that they could absorb pressures on their life. The new view was best expressed by W. V. Grigson, who had a long first hand experience of tribal administration in the Central Provinces and Berar. Grigson held that it was not enough to protect the aboriginal and preserve his institutions; he had to be made fit to hold his own against the rapid growth of civilisation around him and to make his own contribution to the changing life of India and the world at large. But then, the Government had also to take into account the fact that some aboriginals were still in a state of extreme backwardness; and so, if they were "immediately exposed to the full blast of modern conditions", "they would be bound to go to the walls." Opening up these tracts could be counter-productive; besides, each tribal culture had better be seen in its proper relationship with its neighbouring culture and with the general Hindu culture as its background.[51] One uniform tribal policy was difficult to adopt, for there were variations in the development of tribal tracts, in the problems they encountered, in the extent of tribal-non-tribal interaction and their acculturation and finally in the reaction of local men to administrative measures.

Eminent anthropologists, B. S. Guha, D. N. Majumdar, J. P. Singh, F. Bailey and Verrier Elwin, whose services were requisitioned by both the Government of Orissa and Government of India, held the same view as Grigson. Guha made a distinction between involuntary transformation of tribal life through its willing interaction with non-tribal culture, and tribal-non-tribal conflict caused by administrative measures aiming at reinforcing tribal-non-tribal interaction. He deplored the Government's forest regulations and restrictive game laws which in preventing the outflow of "primitive energies" in the tribal people affected the "gaiety and joy of primitive life."[52] Anthroplogists attributed the disintegration of aboriginal culture to the "want of interest in life and mental apathy" caused among the people by the many restrictive measures of the Government itself. They even struck a note of warning against Christian missionary activities in tribal tracts :

> It is a dangerous pastime to save the primitive soul by alien methods and religion, for in such attempts, more often than not, the primitive man himself disappears.[53]

For long the tribesmen had indeed suffered an alien administration which did not quite understand their life while seeking to improve it. Most high officers at the policy formulation level did not know any tribal language, and most judges, passing sentences on tribal convicts, did not take into account tribal customs, traditions and tribal psyche. Rejecting the supposed correlation between drunkenness and tribal crime, Elwin asserted that any interference with the aboriginals' drinking habits amounted to an attack on their life itself, for the "life of the aboriginal depends so entirely on certain stimulants to existence that without them he quickly loses the desire to live."[54]

When the aboriginal came out of jail after serving the sentence for a crime committed while drunk, "his faith in life gets broken" with his "nature permanently twisted".[55] The availability of cheap liquor in tribal tracts thanks to arrack contractors and distillers brought in by the Government increased drunkenness in the aboriginals besides making the traditional home brewing uneconomic; in consequence, many rites and rituals associated with the brewing of liquor in tribal homes were abandoned,[56] the jest of life itself having been affected.

Elwin doubted if even education could remove crimes in tribal tracts, for with education had appeared new forms of crime, not typically tribal—blackmailing, impersonation and cheating, for example.[57] J. P. Singh, a noted anthropologist, saw, like both British and Indian Agency officers, the Kandhs having imbibed from the *dombos* the habit of telling lies frequently.[58] "Civilisation" had taken its toll in other forms as well: syphilis raged in Ganjam tribal tracts[59] following prostitution encouraged by merchants and contractors of the plains. Some local officers' discouragement of tribal feasts and dances with some sexual orgies accompanying them prevented the dancers' "artistic outlet" besides making the wearing of some special dresses and ornaments on such occasions no longer necessary; this also affected the display of tribal talent in both making such dresses and wearing them.[60] The anthropologists cautioned the Government against "uplifting the aborigines by emasculation", which could " never compensate for a vigorous tribal life even it was based on different moral and religious standards from those of civilised men."[61] The anthropologists wanted civilisation to gently seep through tribal life, not swamp it, so that the aboriginal man gets " a breathing time and sufficient space to adjust himself" with the new environment "in his own time and in his own way".[62]

Both administrators and anthroplogists confirmed the emergence of new centres of economic power and new methods of acquiring it in tribal tracts. Despite the Government's ban on *podu* by non-tribals, Oriya settlers practised it extensively to grow new crops on hill slopes. They brought hemp to the Ganjam Agency where the Kandhs had no knowledge of it before.[63] The *panas*, traditionally the minions of the Kandhs and parasites on them, acquired wealth by money-lending and land grabbing, not abandoning, however, their traditional occupation—weaving and peddling goods. Agency officers noted the growing economic power of the *panos* and their tendency to exploit the Kandhs and Savaras. They charged the tribals three-four times more than the bazar rates; they purchased from the Kandhs green plantains very cheap, ripened them artificially and sold them in market below hills and earned a large profit.[64] Some Oriyas let out hill slopes to *panos* and *paiks* who produced crops there and sold them in the markets. These *panos* and *paiks* often engaged tribal labour for clearing hill slopes for cultivation, paying the men either a pittance or nothing at all, claiming the service as the traditional *bethi*. And this when the Government's conservation policy had left the tribals with little land for *podu*[65] and regulations existed banning *podu* by non-tribals. Kandhs paid a high price for cheap cloth brought to the local markets by Telugu traders. Fruit bearing plantation was a development which benefited a few Kandhs; they farmed out their orange trees to *panos* who sold the fruits in markets away from tribal tracts; the panos kept for themselves much of the sale proceeds, giving the Kandhs only a small amount of money.[66] The untouchable *dombos* embraced Christianity and acquired new status and respectability in some Savara tracts. Called *peshnias,* they were the advisers of the tribesmen, and their clout was so extensive as to include in later years even some "political careerists" in Savara tracts.[67]. Even some *bissoyis* were indebted to them who often incited the Savaras to agitate for more lands for *podu,* creating problems for the local administration. Some *dombos* became *paiks* of *bissoyis,* holding rent-free lands and even demanding *mamuls* from the tribals, deepening the latter's discontent.

The Government of Orissa was acutely conscious of the growing problems in the Ganjam Agency; it sought Verrier Elwin's expert opinion on how to tackle the problems. Elwin toured through Ganjam and Koraput tribal tracts in 1943 and 1946.[68] He was in favour of "a gradual and very cautious change" in tribal life,[69] which tended to get vulgarised in proportion as it was being modernised. He would carefully conserve the distinctiveness of the tribal culture and tradition; in his view administration needed to adjust itself to tribal life rather than the latter be moulded to suit administrative needs.

Elwin was happy that for the aboriginals of Ganjam Assam tea gardens had indeed been "an area of adventure",[70] and service in

Mesopotemia a wholesome experience. He saw several indicators of their changed outlook. Lanjia Savara women wore singlets and saris; beef-eating among some tribals was "suffering the reluctant pangs of abdication", and village dormitories going underground.[71] But this was a superficial, no real, change. The aboriginals of Ganjam and Koraput were the same conservative and unchanging people in their religious and general outlook. Women, for example, still tattooed their body and opposed marriage outside clan. The men had imbibed only the external aspect of western civilisation; they wore torn jerseys and trousers for "prestige", no matter, if never being washed at all, they caused skin diseases to the wearers. Human sacrifice had justification in the Kandh mind not only for good crops but to avert tiger menace as well. They were the same as ever, the "most difficult, timid and suspicious" of all tribes, their traditional aversion to education remaining intact.[72]

Even the second world war had made "astonishingly little difference" to the aboriginal life. Very few people knew of the war at all while most dreaded the flying aircrafts as omens of death and disease. A few bold ones, however, held the aircrafts in awe and reverence. "for they were the vehicles of Queen Victoria who flies over from the other world to see if all is well in the Ganjam hills."[73]

Even those who had held Government service for years and had been through a steady process of acculturation with "civilised" men in offices clung to their accustomed values of life. Elwin saw their homes as dark, stuffy and untidy as ever before. Many tribes, though living in the same tract for ages, continued with their habitually exclusive living, Kandhs and Savaras alone interacting in some measure; most Savara villages had pillars representing the *meriah* diety, although the tribe had never practised the rite.[74]

The destruction and decay of aboriginal crafts and industries worried all anthropologists; "inartistic" mill cloth had been fast replacing "the durable and artistic cloth" of the Gadabas made from the fibre of a local deciduous plant, it being the very "badge of the tribe."[75]

Elwin, once an ardent Gandhite and an advocate of *khadi,* berated Congress "misguided reformers" who, during the Quit India movement, had tried to discourage the tribal bark-cloth home industry with a view to popularising *khadi* in Gadaba tracts. The half-hearted attempt of some Gadabas to grow cotton, spin *khadi* and launch an "unfamiliar industry" dismally failed; the men were excommunicated by the tribal council. The Congress reformist zeal thus created a group of Gadabas "who have lost their very useful home industry and who are now regarded as untouchables by their fellows." Similar was Elwin's reaction to popularise *khadi* among the Bondos and Parongos. He wondered why Congressmen urged Gadaba women to wear nose rings—like the untouchable *dombo* women—and not ear rings as had been their traditional adornment; he was not too sure if Congressmen recognised the nose rings as the easier means of leading the Gadabas "by their nose".[76]

Elwin was upset by the sight of "wholesale robbery and exploitation" of the aborigines; he was "sickened and exasperated by tales of cheating and oppression" of the men by local non-tribals and even Government employees, despite the many rules and regulations to protect tribal interests. Tribal land alienation went on unabated as did tribal indebtedness, each causally related to the other. Most local officers knew no tribal language whatever; only a few liked postings in tribal tracts; all others having such postings against their will tried for quick transfer; and none was unaware of the hordes of "corrupt and worthless" *peshnias* prowling the Agency, and *biossyis* and *paiks* like "raging lions" tearing tribal life to tatters.[77]

Little wonder, Elwin felt relieved seeing the absence of "civilisation" in the hills of the Ganjam Agency, "an unusually free country" where no land revenue settlement prevailed and where the forest staff had been posted only very recently. Elwin noted — though with no great disappointment—the "quite shocking state of man power and utter indifference of the people to the elementary amenities of living".[78] Elwin, strongly opposed to interference with tribal life, wanted no ban on axe cultivation even in hill tracts inhabited by the Kandhs and Savaras, for it was their "subsidiary means of livelihood" and but "a symptom of a certain stage of cultural development" which would disappear of itself when the stage would pass. Any Government interference with it now would cause "psychological damage" to the tribals and might even stimulate "their deep-rooted hostility to Government."[79]

Unlike in the Kandh tracts below hills, where excise regulations prevailed, drunkenness was no problem in hill tracts where no such regulations existed.[80] The local Kandhs drank their home brewn liquor and enjoyed all the festivities associated with its making.

The new post-independence government of Orissa was convinced that tribal life to improve needed the inculcation of a new administrative spirit itself, and that called for a new view of tribal values. The aboriginals had indeed been treated so long "as a sort of an animal, wild and savage and not really quite worthwhile" with the result that he had naturally viewed the Government as more "an evil necessity" than "a positive agency of welfare," so lamented F. Bailey, who knew the Kandhs intimately for many years.[81] For tribal administration to succeed, the men needed to be respected, while being governed, advised Elwin.[82]

The advice went home—for the moment at least. Thus both Udaynath Patnaik[83] and J. N. Mohanty,[84] early Oriya officers to report on Ganjam tribal tracts and their problems after independence, stressed the urgency of treating the tribals differently from the way they had been treated till 1947. Mohanty pointed out:

> the long-neglected aboriginals do not by any means belonged to a sub-human species of the human race nor they are in need of protection for all times.[85]

What alone was necessary was to provide them with opportunities and facilities so that they could grow in material and moral stature to take their rightful place in the bodypolitic of the country without any risk of exploitation by their neighbours or of "economical and physical extinction."[86]

British tribal administration had chiefly been of a "negative character", Mohanty correctly observed, the Government's efforts having been restricted to "isolated efforts to prevent the exploitation of the aborigines" and dissuading them from their bad habits and practices and disturbing by violent means peace and order. The only positive feature of the British tribal administration had been the very limited introduction of education and public health. The British government believed in "light administration", non-interference with tribal life being its basic feature. Naturally, therefore, it had made no efforts to raise the tribals to the level of non-tribals, politically and economically, so as to "make them fit for the impact of civilisation" and "take their rightful place in the changing socio-political and economic life of the country". Such a people as left by the British administration could not quite fit in with the situation in independent India where self-governing institutions had been functioning.[87]

The British government had always treated the tribals as isolates, protected wards under perpetual tutelage. Even the engagement of pleaders by tribals involved in court cases was frowned upon by the authorities, who wanted the men to look to Government officers alone for any redressal of their grievances. Pleaders fleecing the ignorant and gullible tribals was, of course, a factor influencing the Government's ban on pleaders, but fear of political influence growing in the tribals through some nationalist minded pleaders was also a factor.[88]

The scope of administration having been widened by the independent Indian government, and the concept of the general welfare of all segments of population underlying administration at all levels, many features of the British tribal administration were found wholly incompatible with the needs of the changed times. Some old familiar institutions in the Ganjam Agency were successively done away with—*mamul, bethi* and finally, the *muthadari* system itself, for example. Administrative necessity was now no excuse for retaining those features of the aboriginal administration which were patently unjust and morally degrading. Both the *mamul* and *bethi* were feudal institutions which had kept the tribals in bondage for decades; the Government had now no need for *muthadars,* prepared as it was for taking direct charge of the tribals. In the paternal administration of the British the aboriginals had been kept under the protective wings of the Government; in the democratic government of independent India, the tribals, still toddlers, were set on their own feet and encouraged to step out into the wide world to gain experiences, both encouraging and despairing.

Notes and References

1. The authority of the Madras government on the Ganjam district and the tribal tracts in it ended in 1936 when they formed a part of the newly created province of Orissa.
2. Problems in the Agency tracts were discussed in annual Agency conferences and measures suggested to tackle them. GC, Deptt. of Land Revenue. D. Dis./835/1934. *Ibid.*, Land Revenue and Salt Deptt. D. Dis./7597/1931.
3. *Ibid.*, R. Dis./1903/1934; 3611/1932.
4. The Rayagada *bissoyi* was "like a slave to the Pano leader to whom the whole of the muttah was practically mortgaged.", *Ibid.* 3885/1932.
5. *Ibid.* D. Dis. 2705/1931.
6. Report on the Ganjam Agency, 1947, Pt. I, by Udaynath Patnaik. The Excise rule was amended in about 1915. GC, Deptt. of Land Revenue. D. Dis. 1835/ 1934. *Ibid.* Deptt. of Revenue, R. D. 3518/1936.
7. Udaynath Patnaik's Report, *op. cit.;* J. N. Mohanty, *A Report on the Mamools in Ganjam Agency,* 1952 (Cuttack, 1952).

8. GC., Deptt. of Revenue, R. D. 3519/1936. The Government fixed rates for carrying luggages.

9. Local officers noticed "abnormal variation" between the *mamul* rates prevailing and those settled in Taylor's *memorandum* in 1902. G. C. R. Dis. 591/1930, Vol. I. Taylor had settled the rates of *mamul* and *bethi* when there was unrestricted *podu* and no reserved forests, the two measures which upset the traditional economic life in the Agency tracts.

10. In stressing this unfortunate state of affairs, the Agency office noted : "We are working willing horses to their death and leaving the unruly ones serving alone." GC. D. Dis. 1835/1934. By this time, the Christian Panas' reluctance to do *bethi* had already created problems for the local authorities of the Agency administration. *Ibid.,* 3985/1932.

11. *Ibid.,* 6756/1926. Also Madras Govt., Govt. Order No. 1456, Judicial, 19 Sept. 1868.

12. The 1917 Act prohibiting tribal land alienation was practically a dead letter. Compared to the tribals in Ganjam, those of the neighbouring Vizag Agency made more effective use of the Act. GC. D. Dis. 1835/1934.

12a. The matter figured prominently in the annual Agency conferences which were attended by the Commissioner of Land Revenue, Govt. of Madras, besides high officers of the Excise, Revenue and Public Works Deptts. GC. Dis. 1921/1926; Di. Dis. 1835/1934.

13. The Ganjam Agent held that the case for ryotwari settlement was not imminent nor was the time favourable for its introduction. He viewed it as particularly inadvisable to weaken the influence of the *bissoyis* and enter into direct relations with ryots for revenue collection. It was only with the help of *bissoyis* and their retainers, "who were more or less immune from malaria" that the Government could "exercise a continuous and effective control over the Savaras." *Ibid.*

13a. Madras Govt, Govt. Order No. 367, Educational, 31 May 1905: Director of Public Instruction, Madras to Chief Secretary, 16 May 1905. In 1894-5, there were 526 Kandh boys out of 2356 in Agency schools; in 1905, the number was 1698 out of 3858 in Government and aided schools in the Agency, which indicated only a "satisfactory advance on paper", because most Kandh boys left schools before passing even the primary standard. In 1933, the Agent reported that probably eighty per cent of the "educated" tribals soon relapsed to illiteracy. GC. D. Dis. 1835/1934.

14. J. C. Molony, Special Asst. Agent, Baliguda Division, to the Agent, 28 Apr. 1904 in Govt. Order, 367, Educational, 31 May 1905, *op. cit.*

15. *Ibid.*

16. Molony to Chief Secretary, 28 Apr. 1905, *Ibid.*

17. GC. D. Dis. 1835/1934, *op. cit.*

18. Govt. of Madras, Rev. Deptt. Govt. Order, Revenue, 2069, 13 Nov. 1933, enclosing Ganjam Agency Administration Report, 1932-33 (Tamil Nadu Archives).

18a. Education officers repeatedly admitted that tribal education had little relevance to tribal economic life, GC. 330/1904 : Gopinath Panigrahi, Superintendent of Hill Schools, Surada, to Agent, 23 Dec. 1904. From 1920 to 1930, 76 Savaras and 64 non-Savaras (mainly Oriyas and Panas) were employed as teachers in Agency schools. Madras Govt. Order, Revenue No. 2461, 19 Nov. 1931, enclosing Ganjam Agency Administration Report, 1930-1. In 1931-2 Administration Report it was also pointed out that educated tribals wanted to be school teachers only. Since schools were not too many, the educated tribals remained unemployed. Madras Govt. Order, Revenue No. 2152, 21 Oct. 1932. The Agent reported that "the economic inducement is therefore becoming less, and elementary education in the higher schools may soon receive a definite set back." Madras Govt. Order, Revenue, No. 2059, 23 Nov. 1933, enclosing Agency. Admn. Report, 1932-3.

19. GC. D. Dis. 1835/1934, *op. cit.*

20. GC. R. D. 3519/1936 : J. N. Mishra, Special Asstt. Agent, Baliguda and S. D. O. Kandhmals, to Deputy Commissioner, Kandhmals, 27 July 1940.

21. Administration Report of the Ganjam Agency, 1883-84.

22. Madras Govt. Order, Revenue, No. 2461, 19 Nov. 1931, Agency Administration Report, 1930-31.

23. GC. R. Dis. 591/1930, Vol. I and R. Dis. 2352/1932.

24. Madras Govt. Order, Miscellaneous Revenue, No. 3217, 27 May 1890.

25. Mounsey, Special Asstt. Agent , found the Ghumsur hill Kandhs "wasting money in litigation", and the local Panas encouraging them. H. Mounsey, *op. cit.*

25a. "The Savaras are losing their well known respect for veracity and trying to wriggle out of their legitimate obligations to render *vetti* and give mamul". GC. R. Dis. 2627/1933 : P. S. Vishanath Ayyar, Asstt. Agent, Baliguda, to Agent, 21 June 1934.

26. GC. R. Dis. 1903/1934.

27. *Census of India, 1921, Vol. XIII: Ganjam, Pt. I,* by G. T. Boag (Madras, 1922), p. 41.

28. *Ibid., 1911, Vol. XII, Madras,* by Charles Molony (Madras, 1912), p. 63.

29. Madras Govt. Order, Revenue No. 2461, 19 Nov. 1933, Agency Administration Report, 1930-31. Elwin saw some Kandhs having adopted the Hindu custom of burning those who died of disease rather than burying them, their accustomed practice. *Man in India*, XXIV, Mar. 1944, No. 1., pp. 51-53.

30. GC. R. Dis. 591/1930, Vol. I.

31. GC. R. Dis. 4197/1931.

31a. GC. C-2967/1921-S-3.

32. *Census of India, 1911, op. cit.*, p. 63.

33. GC. R./ D. 3519/1936, *op. cit.* Also Udaynath Patnaik's Report, *op. cit.*

34. G. C. R. D. 3519/1936, *op. cit.*

35. Udaynath Patnaik's Report, *op. cit.*

36. GC. 3555/1925.

37. Atul Chandra Pradhan, "A Study of the Political Movement in Nilgiri in the Wider Context of the Indian Nationalist Movement", *J. O. H.*, Vol V. Jan. 1983, No. 1, pp. 25-40. Praharaj, *op. cit.*, pp. 129-53. Atul Chandra Pradhan and Ashok Kumar Patnaik, eds., *People's Movements in Orissa During the Colonial Era.* (Post-Graduate Deptt. of History, Utkal University, Vani Vihar, Bhubaneshwar, 1994), pp. 62-97.

38. Madras Govt. Order, Revenue No. 2152, Ganjam Agency Administration Report, 1931-2. Atul Chandra Pradhan and Ashok Kumar Patnaik, *op. cit.*, p. 165.

39. Prasanna Kumar Mishra, "Tribal Resistance Movement in Orissa", *Ibid*, p. 17..

40. Madras Govt. Order, Revenue No. 2461, 19 Nov. 1931. Ganjam Agency Administration Report, 1930-31.

41. Madras Govt. Order, Revenue (Special Dept., No. 227, 4 Feb. 1920; Govt. Order, Revenue, No. 2461, 19 Nov. 1931 : Ganjam Agency Administration Report, 1930-31. GC. C-2967/1921, *op. cit.*

42. *Ibid.* Verrier Elwin, *A Brief Survey of the Aboriginal Tribes of the Districts of Ganjam and Koraput* (Cuttack, 1946), p. 4.

43. *Ibid.*

44. That is high caste people. GC. C-2967, *op. cit.*

45. *Ibid.*

46. *Ibid.*

47. *Ibid.*

48. *Report on the Partially Excluded Areas Enquiry Committee* (Cuttack, 1940), pp. 3, 10. Shri A. V. Thakkar of the Harijan Sevak Sanstha was the Chairman of the Committee.

49. GC. 2761-A 31959 : S. B. Panda, Sub-Deputy Collector and Magistrate, Parlakimedy, to Agent, Ganjam, 29 Nov. 1938.

50 *Ibid.*

51. W. V. Grigson, *The Aboriginal Problem in the Central Provinces and Berar* (Nagpur, 1944). Also *Man in India*, XXIV, June 1944, No. 2, pp. 67-68.

52. *Ibid.* XXIV, September 1944, No. 3, p. 136.
53. *Ibid.*
54. *Ibid.* , XXIV, March 1944, No. 1, p. 60.
55. *Ibid.*
56. *Ibid.*, p. 61.
57. *Ibid.*
58. J. S. Singh, *Social Service Quarterly,* XXX, p. 128. Also *Man in India,* XXIV, March 1944. No. 1, pp. 62-63.
59. GC. Dis. 1835/1934, *op. cit.*
60. *Man in India,* XXIV, September, 1944, No. 3, Comment, pp. 138-40.
61. *Ibid.*, p. 140.
62. *Ibid.*
63. GC. R. D. 3519/1936, *op. cit.* By an Act of 1905, non-tribals were prohibited from *podu.*
64. GC. R. Dis. 591/1930, Vol. 1. *Ibid.*, 3611/1932. Verrier Elwin, "Notes on a Khond Tour", *Man in India,* XXIV, March 1944, No. 1, pp. 57-59.
65. *Ibid.*
66. *Ibid.*
67. Gopinath Mohanty, "Fading Outlines in a Tribal Culture", Bined S. Das, *ed.*, *Life and Culture in Orissa* (Calcutta, 1984), p. 203.
68. Elwin, *Notes . . . . Tour, op. cit.* and his *A Brief Survey ... Koraput, op. cit.*
69. *Ibid.*, p. 20.
70. *Ibid.*, p. 3.
71. *Ibid.*, p. 4.
72. *Ibid.*, p. 16.
73. *Ibid.*, p. 4.
74. *Ibid.*, p. 5.
75. *Ibid.*, pp. 14-15.
76. *Ibid.*
77. *Ibid.*, p. 11.
78. *Man in India,* XXIV, March 1944, No. 1, Elwin's article, *op. cit.*, p. 57.
79. Elwin, *A Brief Survey, op. cit.*, p. 7.
80. Elwin saw "temperance and absence of drunkenness in the Orissa hills". The highlanders were "surprisingly moderate in their use of alcohol.", *Ibid.*, p. 4.
81. See his *Caste and Economic Frontier : A Village in Highland Orissa* (Manchester, 1957), p. 12.

82. His *Brief Survey, op. cit.*, p. 20.

83. He wrote a report on the Ganjam Agency in 1947 describing the kinds of *mamuls* prevalent there. The evils of *bethi* were also stressed by him.

84. He also submitted a report on the *mamuls* in the Ganjam Agency in 1952. He held that the *muthadari* system had outlived its purpose.

85. *Ibid.*

86. *Ibid.*

88. *Ibid.*. In 1934, the Agent disapproved the engagement of Umacharan Patnaik, a leading lawyer of Berhampur and later an M. P. by the tribals of R. Udaygiri in a case involving *mamul*. The Special Asst. Agent was asked to settle the dispute. GC. D. Dis. 3264/1934.

Conclusion

British rule in tribal regions changed the local life, the pace and the extent of change varying between regions. The change was at places and on occasions consciously effected by the rulers; at others it was the result of circumstances created by no calculated official policy. Both the scale and scope of change in tribal life depended as much on local reaction to it as on the keenness or otherwise of the rulers to bring the change about; and the keenness, in its turn, depended on what the general nature of the local men was as also on how important the men and their tract were in the rulers' view.

The change in tribal life followed at times and at places just the lines the rulers had drawn while at others it took a course far different from what the rulers had intended. The change in tribal life followed no uniform or consistent pattern even in the same tract, for local circumstances differed.

The varied nature of the change in tribal life marked both the success and failure of the British tribal policy, the test being the nature, intensity and duration of the tribal response to the measures of change; and the response varied between stubborn resistance, grudging acquiescence and willing acceptance.

Just as tribal reactions to administrative measures varied between even sections of the same tribal society, so did the views of the administrators themselves on the measures most likely to be successful and those that were doomed to failure. Official papers make this clear.

The British government and its tribal subjects learned from their respective experience, the latter ultimately resigning themselves to externally-induced change as an inexorable development in their life, while the former realised that in dealing with the aborigines, it was wise to mark time and hasten slowly. Over the years the interaction between the British rulers and their functionaries on the one hand and the tribals on the other influenced their mutual attitude. Abandoning their earlier policy of reclaiming the tribal society and religion, the British would later conserve and even revive tribalism, recognising a clear correlation between modernisation of tribal institutions and vulgarisation of their life. At the end of the British rule there was a virtual turn about in the British tribal policy from one of "civilising the barbarians" by alternate coercion and conciliation to protecting the "noble savages" by a paternalistic administration with *laissez faire* as its general note.

Generally speaking, contact with the tribals was the result of campaigns against them; then followed a gradual control of tribal life which disturbed its traditional tenor. British authority interposed itself between the tribals and their accustomed rulers, the non-tribal *rajas* and the zamindars. The traditionally close bond between them was not snapped, but the British government made sure that the bond furthered its interests rather than harmed them. British administrative measures gradually weakened the pre-eminence of the traditional non-tribal elite in tribal polity and society; the aboriginals saw for themselves that many of their *rajas* and zamindars had been cowed into quiescence by both British arms and diplomacy while some others, by temptation, made willing allies and obliging accomplices of the new rulers to promote, protect and preserve their interests.

The tribals had no earlier experience of a strong and regular administration which impinged on their accustomed life in many ways. British rule stopped the endemic feuds and bloody inter-clan skirmishes; peace and order was established no doubt, but, from the tribal point of view, it damaged tribal society : fights and feuds constituted the traditional test of tribal leadership, besides being the essential unifying factor for individual clans. They were a means of toning up both the physical strength and moral fibre of local men. Both British anthropologists and administrators recognised in later years a clear correlation between the want of manliness in the tribes and their peaceful and orderly life structured by the British government itself.

Gradually, codified and definite rules and regulations replaced the customary tribal usages and practices; courts interpreted the rules and regulations strictly as the police implemented them vigorously, weakening in the process the traditional authority of tribal patriarchs. Local disputes could no longer be settled locally, a development which British officers themselves regretted later when they saw ignorant and credulous tribals being fleeced by pleaders. Tribal outbreaks had much to do with the misuse of power by the lower echelons of the administration itself; official reports made clear that the appurtenances of a modern civilised administration could hit tribal interests hard.

The British government's economic measures also had grave implications for tribal life. The policy of conserving forests and controlling shifting cultivation, for example, led to migration of tribals to unfamiliar tracts when life became difficult in their own accustomed habitat. The leasing of forests to railway sleeper contractors, the establishment of marts and fairs in tribal tracts and the gradual replacement of the traditional subsistence economy by market economy brought into tribal tracts a stream of non-tribal people who had little in common with the local people. A conflict of interests between the local people and the immigrants lay in the very logic of circumstances. The newmen made the most of the British administration, acting often as collaborators of the official functionaries to exploit the local people. Often there were tensions in tribal society between groups who profited by their close nexus with the new extraneous elements brought in by the Government and those, local tribal leaders, who shunned the elements as the despoilers of tribal interests. British administration aggravated divisions in tribal society; some tribal groups with closer interaction with non-tribals profited by the new economic opportunities opened by the local administration; some others, who avoided such interaction, lagged economically far behind. Tribal impoverishment inevitably followed tribal land alienation. For the aggrieved tribals revolts against their despoilers became risky, roads built by the Government, mostly with ill-paid or free tribal labour, having broken the inaccessibility of many tracts. The aboriginals sank into sullen acquiescence—a development which the British officers, especially the local ones, sincerely deplored, especially because they could do practically nothing to stem the process.

Tribal—non-tribal acculturation was a process which antedated the British rule of the tribal tracts, but the process had been an unobtrusive one for centuries, the result of no consciously adopted policy of any ruling authority before. Under the British rule, such acculturation was a deliberately adopted policy of the Government for a time. It was hard for the tribals to adjust themselves to either the pace or the extent of acculturation encouraged by the British administration. Later, however, the Government recognised the socio-economic problems created by the non-tribal immigrants and settlers in tribal tracts; but then, the official reaction to this issue even then could be only ambivalent : the process could neither be reversed nor could the administrators wink at the havoc it had caused to tribal life. The Government's measures had created in the tribal people new economic wants but with no commensurate increase in their means to meet them. Local British officers admitted that the general degradation of tribal life had been coeval, commensurate and co-extensive with the consolidation of the British administration itself. The fact that the agencies of change in tribal life had turned themselves into agents of exploitation of the life itself was a point repeated in official reports of the 1930s and later.

As for the official policy of "civilising the savages", the British could claim but a limited success. The public performance of inhuman rites and practices was stopped no doubt, but the tribal mind continued to find a causal connection between the stoppage of the practices and the wrath of their deities in the form of droughts and epidemics. The tribal mind did not change despite the Government's educational programme spanning many decades.

Periodical revolts in tribal tracts led to a shift of emphasis in the tribal policy, though not in the policy itself as such. Government interests would now have to be reconciled with tribal fears and hopes; tribal reaction would now measure the merit of any scheme for tribal uplift. The civilising mission was, of course, not given up; only its pace was slowed down and its scope carefully considered. Stricter control was imposed on Government functionaries in tribal tracts and greater accountability was insisted upon to prevent any gross misuse of power by them. The government was now far keener to safeguard tribal interests, many local officers even crying halt to some ongoing measures. The Government was far more sensitive to tribal feelings and susceptibilities as indicated by its regular monitoring of tribal reactions to the administrative measures adopted in their tracts.

Change in tribal character followed their increasing exposure to "civilisation". Deceit and falsehood, aversion to hard work and even propensity to gain at the cost of follow tribals were clear indicators of the process of detribalisation; the change in tribal character was most apparent in tracts where the influence of the "civilised" administration was the greatest and where tribal-non-tribal acculturation had been most prolonged and most intimate. But then, there also grew in some tribals, converts to Christianity, particularly, a spirit of assertiveness against authority and reluctance to meekly suffer exploitation; this did cause some problems for the local administration which had so long been accustomed to abject docility in most aboriginals. Some officers frankly admitted the fact of administrative inconvenience caused by what they also viewed as the trend of moral elevation of the tribals.

Conserving tribalism became from around the late 1930s both a cultural policy and political necessity of the British government. The Government was now keen to keep the tribals away from the contaminating contact of politically restive people in non-tribal districts that abutted on tribal tracts. Now many anthropologists and administrators deplored the progressive loss of traditional tribal values as a result of the Government's earlier mission of civilising the savages. But then, it was now too late to reverse the trend of detribalisation; at most its pace could be controlled and its general effect regulated.

Wholly different was the attitude of the Indian nationalists who wanted integration of the tribals in the political and cultural mainstream of the Indian people at large. Conservation of tribalism was to them a wholly regressive measure for any Government to adopt; the British tribal policy appeared to Indian nationalists as a sinister and devious scheme of keeping up the tribal-non-tribal divide with a view to furthering the colonial interests of the British. No wonder in the Orissa Legislative Assembly the British tribal policy came in for criticism, and the first Congress ministry (1937-39) made an enquiry into the condition prevalent in tribal tracts, declared Partially Excluded Areas under the Government of India Act, 1935. Administrators, however, had a mixed feeling on how to go about the tribal problem, some urging the protection of tribal identity, some others favouring closer and quicker integration of the tribals with the non-tribals for the former's own uplift.

The British left their Indian successors with the same problem they had faced and which they could not solve themselves : whether to let the tribals go about their own accustomed way or to regulate their way of life with a view to changing it for the better. The independent Indian government clearly saw the inverse relationship between administrative measures for tribal uplift and persistence of the values cherished by the tribals themselves. Tribal welfare formed an important part in the Government's scheme of national development; but then, the tribal policy needed to be implemented in such a way as not to cause misgivings in the aboriginal mind if the Government's welfare measures squared well with the tribals' own concept of their material and moral progress. Today these misgivings underlie the widening Naxalite movement in parts of

Andhra Pradesh bordering tribal tracts of Orissa. The movement has driven home an important point : the proclaimed policy of tribal welfare is worth nothing if the agency charged with its implementation is found wanting in both aptitude and ability to do the job. Indeed, it is the men in the tribal administration at lower levels that matter the most, not the measures for tribal welfare formulated at high levels of the Government.

Bibliography

Unpublished Material

New Delhi, National Archives of India

Records of the Home (Public) Department of the Government of India, 1840-62.

Records of the Foreign (Political) Department of the Government of India - A Proceedings, 1882.

Nagpur, Madhya Pradesh Old Secretariat Record Room

Letters from the Chief Commissioner, Central Provinces to the Government of India, 1864-1884.

Letters from the Government of India to the Chief Commissioner, Central Provinces, 1864-1884.

Foreign Department (Political) Proceedings, Government of India, 1870-82.

Calcutta, West Bengal Archives

Judicial (Criminal) Department Proceedings of the Government of Bengal, 1840-60.

Political Department Consultation of the Government of Bengal, 1859

Political Department Proceedings of the Government of Bengal, 1863.

Madras (now Chennai), Tamil Nadu Archives

Judicial Department Proceedings of the Government of Madras, 1864-1936.

Proceedings of the Director of Public Instruction, Madras, 1870-1936.

Proceedings of the Revenue Department, Government of Madras, 1890-1900.

Reports on the Administration of Public Affairs in the Madras Presidency for the years 1855-56 and for 1860-61.

Chhatrapur, Ganjam District Collectorate

Correspondence of the Agent, Ganjam Agency with the Government of Madras, 1860-1936.

Published Material

Government Publications

Census of India, 1921, XIII: Ganjam, Pt. 1 (Madras, 1922)
Census of India, 1921, XII: Madras (Madras, 1912)
Report on the Partially Excluded Areas Enquiry Committee (Cuttack, 1940).
Report on the Mamools of Ganjam Agency, by J. N. Mohanty (Cuttack, 1952)
Memorandum on the Ganjam Maliahs, by M. D. Taylor (Reprint, Cuttack, 1949)
Minutes Recorded by Lord Napier (Madras, 1873).
Reports of the Meriah Agents (Ganjam) from 1837 to 1861 (Madras, 1883).
Selections from the Old Records of the Ganjam Collectorate (Chhatrapur, 1936).
History of the Rise and Progress of Operations for the Suppression of Human Sacrifice and Female Infanticide in the Hill Tracts of Orissa, (Calcutta, 1854).
Madras Manual of Administration, 2 Vols. (Madras, 1885)
History of the Ganjam Maliahs : Information regarding the Special Assistant Agent's Division, by H. Mounsey (Madras, 1884).
Minutes Recorded by Baron Napier During his Administration of the Madras Presidency from 1866 to 1872 (Madras 1873).
Report on the Bissoyis of Parlakhamundi, by C. F. McCartie, 24 November 1881.
Ganjam District Manual, by T. J. Maltby (Madras 1918).
Manual of the District of Vizagapatnam, by D. F. Carmaichael (Madras, 1869).
Report Upon the Khonds of the Districts of Ganjam and Cuttack, by S. C. Macpherson (Calcutta, 1842).
Report on the Ganjam Agency by Udaynath Patnaik (Cuttack, 1947).

Secondary Sources

Anonynmous, *The Calcutta Review,* VIII, Nos. XV & XVI (July-December, 1847).
Bailey, F. G., *Caste and the Economic Frontier : A Village in Highland*

Orissa (Manchester, 1957).

Bailey, F. G., "Political Change in the Khondmals", *The Eastern Anthropologist,* XI, No.2 (December 1957-February 1958).

Boal, Barbara M. *The Church in the Kond Hills* (1963).

Boal, Barbara M. *The Konds : Human Sacrifice and Religious Change* (Warminister, Wilte, 1982).

Campbell, John, *Narrative by Major General John Campbell of his Operations in the Hill Tracts of Orissa for the Suppression of Human Sacrifice and Female Infanticide* (London, 1861).

Campbell, John, *A Personal Narrative of Thirteen Years' Service Among the Wild Tribes of Khondlistan* (London, 1864).

Carey, S. Pearce, *Dawn on the Kond Hills* (London, 1936).

Dalton, E. T., *Descriptive Ethnology of Bengal* (Indian Reprint, Calcutta, 1973).

Das, Arati, "Female Infanticide in Western India during nineteenth Century" (Unpublished M. Phil dissertation, University of Bombay, 1988).

Duff, Rev. Dr. G., "Goomsur : The Late War There—The Khonds or Wild Tribes", *Calcutta Review,* V. 1846.

Elwin, Verrier, *A Brief Survey of the Aboriginal Tribes of the Districts of Ganjam and Koraput* (Cuttack, 1946).

Elwin, Verrier, : "Notes on a Kond Tour", *Man in India*, XXIV (March, 1944. No.1)

Elwin, Verrier, *Tribal Myths of Orissa* (London, 1954).

Frye, J. P., "On the Uriya and Kondh Population of Orissa", *Journal of the Royal Asiatic Society of Bengal,* XVII (1859-60).

Grigson, W. V., *The Aboriginal Problem in the Central Provinces and Berar* (Nagpur, 1944).

Iyengar, T. E. R., "Resistance to British Rule in Ganjam, 1766-1858:" (Unpublished Ph. D. thesis, Berhampur University, Berhampur, Orissa, 1976).

Macpherson, S. C., "An Account of the Religion of the Khonds of Orissa", *Journal of the Royal Asiatic Society of Great Britain and Ireland,* XIII (1851-52).

Macpherson, William, *Memorials of Service in India : From the Correspondence of the Late Major Samuel Charteris Macpherson, C. B., Political Agent at Gwalior during the Mutiny and Formerly Employed in the Suppression of Human Sacrifice in Orissa* (London, 1865).

Mahapatra, Madan Mohan, "The Changing Pattern of Tribal Economy in Khandmals"- A study in British Impact", *Proceedings of the*

Seminar on Socio-Economic Life of the Tribals of Orissa during the 19th and early 20th centuries (Khalikote College, Berhampur, 5-6 July, 1981).

Mahapatra, Madan Mohan, "Changing Pattern of Khond Life - A study in British Impact", P. K. Mishra, ed., *Culture, Tribal History and Freedom Movement, Dr. N. K. Sahu Commemoration Volume* (Delhi, 1989).

Mishra, Prasanna Kumar, *Political Unrest in Orissa* (Calcutta, 1983).

Mishra, Prasanna Kumar, "Tribal Movements in Orissa, 1821-1942", Atul Chandra Pradhan & Ashok Kumar Patnaik, eds., *People's Movement in Orissa During the Colonial Era* (Post-Graduate Department of History, Utkal University, Bhubaneswar, 1994).

Mohanty, Gopinath, "Fading outlines in a Tribal Culture", Binod S.Das, ed., *Life and Culture in Orissa* (Calcutta), 1984).

Mojumdar, Kanchanmoy, "Revolt in Kalahandi, 1881-82: Peasant Uprising in a Tribal State", *Osmania Journal of Historical Research* (Department of History, Osmania University, Hyderabad); II, Nos. 1 & 2 (January 1983-December 1985).

Mojumdar, Kanchanmoy, "The Kutiya Kandh Uprising, 1865-66 . Tribal Reaction Against the Oriya Elite", *New Aspects of History of Orissa,* (Department of History, Sambalpur University, Jyotivihar), III.

Mojumdar, Kanchanmoy "The Ganjam Agency, 1839-1900 : Some Problems of Tribal Administration", P. K. Mishra, ed., *Culture, Tribal History and Freedom Movement* (Delhi, 1989).

Mukherjee, Prabhat, *History of Orissa,* Vol. VI (Utkal University, 1964).

Panigrahi, Lalita, *British Social Policy and Female Infanticide in India* (New Delhi, 1972).

Pradhan, Atul Chandra, "A study of the Political Movement in Nilgiri in the Wider Context of the Indian Nationalist Movement", *Journal of Orissan History*, V,. No. 1 (January 1983)

Pradhan, Atual Chandra and Patnaik Ashok Kumar, eds., *People's Movements in Orissa During the Colonial Era* (Bhubaneswar, 1994).

Praharaj, Debendra Mohan, *Tribal Movements and Political History in India A Case Study from Orissa, 1803-1949* (New Delhi, 1988.

Swaro, Dasarathi, *The Christian Missionaries in Orissa. Their Impact on Nineteenth Century Society* (Calcutta, 1990).

Taylor, Rev.W. "On the Language, Manners and Rites of the Khonds", *Madras Journal of Literature and Science,* VII (Madras, 1837).

Journals

The Calcutta Review, X (July-December, 1848).
The Calcutta Christian Observer (April-July 1837).
Man in India, XXIV, (March 1944), No. 1; XXIV, (June 1944), No. 2; September, 1944, No. 1
Social Service Quarterly, XXX.

Index